THE *Life* GIVING HOME *experience*

A 12-Month Guided Journey

SALLY CLARKSON
with Joel Clarkson

**TYNDALE®
MOMENTUM**

*An Imprint of
Tyndale House Publishers, Inc.*

Visit Tyndale online at www.tyndale.com.

Visit Tyndale Momentum online at www.tyndalemomentum.com.

Visit Sally Clarkson at www.sallyclarkson.com, www.momheart.com, and www.wholeheart.org.

Visit Joel Clarkson at www.joelclarkson.com.

Contents

Introduction vii

JANUARY Creating a Framework for Home: Rhythms, Routines,
and Rituals 1

FEBRUARY A Culture of Love: Growing Lifelong Relationships 11

MARCH The Art of the Ordinary: Finding Beauty in Your
Own Backyard 21

APRIL A Heritage of Faith: Engaging with God's Story 31

MAY Days to Commemorate: Marking Growth
with Celebration 41

JUNE Times of Delight: Creating a Value for Play 53

JULY A Heroic Heritage: Engaging with Story and History 65

AUGUST The Story of Us: Shaping and Celebrating
Family Culture 77

SEPTEMBER When Seasons Change: Gathering In for Home
and Soul 87

OCTOBER Home Is Best: Serving Life within Your Walls 97

NOVEMBER Blessed and Blessing: Grace, Gratitude,
and Generosity 107

DECEMBER The Rhythm of Celebration: Seasons of Rejoicing
in Family Life 117

An Invitation to Create a History of Goodness
in Your Home 127
Notes and Ideas 129
About the Authors 131

Introduction

The wise woman builds her house,
But the foolish tears it down with her own hands.

PROVERBS 14:1

I love walking in old neighborhoods. Anytime I visit or move to a new town, one of the first things I do is locate the historical sector, which usually includes an area of delightful century-old homes. I relish the dormer windows, the charming front porches, the ancient trees that guard the lamppost-lined streets.

Every Saturday for eight years straight, my firstborn, Sarah, and I walked the streets in the Old North End neighborhood of Colorado Springs, taking in the beauty and tranquility. It became a rhythm that we practiced with gusto. Later we began to make an annual visit to Asheville, North Carolina, a lovely town tucked away in the Smoky Mountains. All the houses there are a little bit unique—decked out in different hues of vibrant paint, some with turrets or picture windows, most with expansive porches—all designed with the capacity to be inhabited by big, life-loving families. Unlike modern homes, many of which are built identically one after the other, these were constructed with the intention of expressing the creativity and joy of each unique individual and family.

And then, of course, there was Biltmore—the stunning estate outside of Asheville that I describe in *The Lifegiving Home.* Our entire family was captivated by the care and intention George Vanderbilt put into creating a place of great beauty and uniqueness that would serve as a refuge and resource for all who lived and visited and worked there.

Building a home like that requires time and lots of hard work. A great structure never just accidentally comes into being. It starts with careful planning and prep work—acquiring permits, hiring professionals, sourcing materials and fixtures, drawing up blueprints. Then comes the hard work of construction—board by board, brick by brick, paint for each room, adding all the beautiful details that make the home unique. The entire process requires a dedicated intentionality of purpose.

The same is true for you as a home builder—and make no mistake, God designed you to be just that. You may never construct a physical structure to house your family. But you have the God-given call and privilege to plan and establish a home for yourself and those you love—a space and an ambience that serves and shapes the lives of those who inhabit it and those who visit.

A wise woman builds not just her home but also her family narrative, preparing a path of life that will uphold her descendants and give them a foundation of faith. An empowered spiritual home creates a story worth telling for generations to come.

Home building is a capacity God has granted each one of us who learns to walk in His wisdom and skill. However, this great work of home building is a long-term construction project that takes what sometimes seems like endless years of care and hard work. In particular, the formation of the children of a family—nurturing excellent souls, filling minds with truth, inspiring hearts with the purposes of God, instilling a taste for God's goodness and beauty—requires planning and intentionality.

That is the purpose of this planner. Designed as a companion to *The Lifegiving Home*, a book I wrote with Sarah, it provides practical touchpoints for how to implement the ideas introduced in the book and a place to begin writing down your own plans and ideas. Following the pattern of *The Lifegiving Home*, each chapter of this planner focuses on a different month of the year. Each contains the following:

- *A brief introduction* in which I share my heart about the theme for the month. My hope is that in sharing my stories and thoughts I will stimulate your own thinking.
- *At Home in the Word.* This Bible study section touches upon the monthly theme and poses practical questions to stimulate your thinking. There are no right or wrong answers to these questions. The study is intended to inspire your own ideas about how best to realize these precepts.
- *Bringing It Home.* Here I provide some snippets of our family's life over the years—books, movies, family events, and activities that have become part of the Clarkson family heritage. Once again, these are intended to stimulate your own ideas and values, not lay down concrete systems for you to follow. (For more guidance, ask friends for recommendations or refer to the Clarkson family online resource guide at www.lifegivinghome.com.)

Notice that there's space in these chapters to jot down thoughts and plans. You can do this in a separate notebook or journal if you prefer. But I do hope you will read this book with pen poised to write and mind and heart focused to apply its principles to building your home. My heart in this book is that through sharing my soul meanderings about home, I will help you capture a vision and begin to shape a home according to your own convictions.

You don't even have to wait until January to begin. Any month can be your "January" as you renew your commitment to planning and intentionality in building and shaping your home.

I believe in God's willingness to speak into your life and to empower you to craft your home life into a beautiful heritage. May you be blessed as you enter into this journey. Know that I hold a deep thankfulness in my heart that you have decided to step out so bravely into the great beyond of homebuilding.

January

CREATING A FRAMEWORK FOR HOME

Rhythms, Routines, and Rituals

Commit your works to the LORD
And your plans will be established.

PROVERBS 16:3

I can still remember the day. After much deliberation my husband, Clay, and I decided we were going to purchase an empty one-acre lot of mountain land nestled against the foothills of the Rocky Mountains. Thus began the daunting but exhilarating task of constructing our dream home.

Our Rocky Mountain "Rivendell" would provide us with countless happy and meaningful memories during the most important years of our children's youth. But many pieces had to be put in place before that could happen. We had to choose a contractor to oversee the job. Countless choices had to be made regarding paint, carpet, flooring, fixtures, and landscaping. And before we could make any of those decisions, we needed a plan.

When architects consider a house they want to build, they know they must start with a well-crafted, viable blueprint. The blueprint will guide them through all the stages of construction from laying a

1

strong foundation all the way through putting the finishing touches on the building. Even when plans must be changed—as they inevitably are during the process of construction—the blueprint helps guide the adjustments.

So it is with how we create home both physically and spiritually. If we don't have a plan, all the ebbs and flows of life will take us by surprise. All the resources we use to create a home environment will be used on the fly, without a sense of purpose and structure.

So what does a blueprint for a lifegiving home look like? What elements ought to be gathered and considered before setting forth on such a grand and daunting task? This process will look different for every home and family. Every family will set their own pace and find their own rhythms. But as I have observed my own family and the families of friends, I have recognized a few key elements that tend to emerge in every family—things that, if taken into consideration while making a plan, contribute significantly to a positive home environment and help us roll with the punches when changes happen.

First and foremost, figuring out how to manage individual family needs is paramount. It's easy to get caught up in the details and forget that the purpose of a lifegiving home is to nurture real human souls and bodies. Everything else is secondary to this cause.

God interacts with us relationally, as a Parent. He loves each of us and seeks a personal relationship with us. And the best way to create a vibrant life in a home is to do the same—to seek out each individual and relate to that person according to his or her hopes, desires, and needs.

Planning ahead is one of the best ways to ensure every person in the home receives a fair share of attention. Letting our days just happen not only leads to chaos but also increases the chances that what we value most just won't get done.

Certainly every personality interfaces with schedules differently. Some people write out every portion of their day; others take a more general approach. What's important is to invest in planning ahead of time to create space for what matters and to allow for those un-expected moments that inevitably come along.

Managing time is especially important when it comes to creating spaces of calm and restoration. No one can indefinitely manage the whirring machine of the home without taking a break from time to time. Having a rhythm in the home implies that there are both ups and downs, and downtime is a vital part of keeping a good beat. God created the Sabbath as a time to put aside work and instead take a breath and consider Him and His goodness. Not only do we need this weekly Sabbath rest; we need other rest periods as well. For instance, I have found that I need my teatime every afternoon, even if it's only for five minutes. Everyone has a different way of refreshing and restoring their soul. But for most of us, unless we specifically schedule such times of refreshment, they will never happen.

One way to create more space for rest is to keep a close eye on the information that comes into the home. And please note that the issue is not just negative information, but the sheer *amount* of information. E-mails, newsletters, magazines, phone calls—all these things and more can quickly overpower and overwhelm any sense of order and create a sense of chaos. Especially in an era where most people have smartphones at the ready, it is imperative to find a way to limit the flow for both you and your family members. Constantly absorbing incoming information creates a habit of whirlwind living. The only antidote is to be aware of the potential downside of screens of all sorts and other streams of information and plan ahead to create spaces away from those sources.

Like information, *stuff* can quickly create a sense of disorder at home. Clothes, books, dishes, documents, toys, tools, and an assortment of other items pile up so easily in an active family. Modern culture is already bent toward consumerism, and it takes plenty of energy just to buck that trend, not to mention managing the unsightly clutter that results from it.

One great way to fight the clutter and bring more peace into your household is to plan for times when the whole family can participate in straightening and cleaning up. I have found that if I set a timer for ten or fifteen minutes and send each of my family members on lightning cleanup tasks around the house, almost everything gets back to normal. It also helps to schedule an annual house-clearing day, when unused items are gathered and given to Goodwill or the Salvation Army. This is not only a great way to get your kids involved in meaningful giving—it can also make your home feel like a completely new place.

Adding such elements to your home blueprint can ignite an excitement for this stewardship opportunity God has given into your hands. But it's not enough just to plan for these life rhythms; you have to actually practice them, day in and day out. Give yourself grace as you learn new ways of doing life with the ones you love. Adjust your plan as needed and be sure to put your adjusted plan into practice as well. As you persevere, you will begin to see results and relish the world you have created with God's help.

God wants to take the blueprint you design with your family and create a beautiful home out of it. May you entrust yourself and your family to the master Creator, who always finishes the work He begins.

At Home in the Word

1. *"The wise woman builds her house, but the foolish tears it down with her own hands" (Proverbs 14:1).*

    a. What kind of "house" do you want to build in your life? This can be anything from your actual home to your spiritual heritage or even something personal to you. List at least three tools you have for constructing your spiritual/ emotional home.

b. What circumstances or commitments in your life might tempt you to give up or "tear down" your home?

2. *"By wisdom a house is built, and by understanding it is established; and by knowledge the rooms are filled with all precious and pleasant riches" (Proverbs 24:3-4).*

a. What are the sources of wisdom that you can lean on in the creation of your home? Write down at least three ways you want to build wisdom, understanding, and knowledge into your home life. (Note that *wisdom* involves skilled living and could include abilities with relationships, money, time, work, food, decor, and other areas of life.)

b. What influences in your life (foolish voices? temporal values? cultural pressures? old habits?) could potentially keep you from building your home with understanding and knowledge, keep you from gaining wisdom, or compromise your long-term, eternal values? What are the most effective ways to neutralize these influences?

3. *"Unless the LORD builds the house, they labor in vain who build it" (Psalm 127:1).*

    a. God tells us to seek first His Kingdom and His righteousness (Matthew 6:33). How does this apply to the way you build your house? How are you investing in the Word of God in your home? How are you engaging in faith? Righteousness?

    b. Do any aspects of your life feel like they are out of control or could easily become that way? Write them down. Which of these can you intentionally surrender to God, knowing He will take better care of them than you can?

4. *"Delight yourself in the LORD; and He will give you the desires of your heart" (Psalm 37:4).*

    a. What does it mean to delight in God? Write out three ways that you can rest in God and enjoy His presence.

b. What do you desire most? List some of your dearest hopes and dreams. How does your vision for your home connect with these deep desires?

Bringing It Home

What Is Your Biggest Challenge for January?

January has always been a difficult month for me where we live in Colorado. Winter still holds us tightly in its grasp, and we have to endure blizzard after blizzard, awaiting the thaw of spring. To drive the cold away, we love to enjoy warm cups of hot chocolate and gather around the fireplace with a good book to read aloud.

Another challenge for me in January is the process of organization and decluttering I describe in *The Lifegiving Home*. Because I am easily overwhelmed by lots of details, the necessary act of planning for the new year can be daunting. I have learned to rely on Clay's help and support as I do my planning. I have also learned it is important for me to get away and have some quiet time alone during this season. If I make a point to make sure my needs are met during this time, I find the process of planning can be joyful and exciting rather than overwhelming.

What do you struggle with in January? What are you doing (or could you do) to overcome that struggle?

_____

_____

_____

January Anniversaries, Birthdays, and Holidays

January tends to be a quiet time for us regarding family events—a welcome respite from the hustle and bustle of Christmas. However, we like to make an event out of snow days and really take a break from the craziness of normal, day-to-day life. These are special times for making memories and simply enjoying one another's company.

List your own family events for January:

_____

_____

_____

_____

_____

To Read or Watch in January

Picture Books: Oliver Hunkin's *Dangerous Journey* (1985) is an appropriate book for starting out the year. An illustrated adaptation of John Bunyan's allegory, *The Pilgrim's Progress*, it outlines the quest of our hero, Pilgrim, to find the heavenly city.

Literature and Nonfiction: *Little Britches* (1950) is Ralph Moody's quaint autobiographical tale of his early years on a ranch in Littleton, Colorado, at the beginning of the twentieth century.

Movies and Series: Every year for many years, we gathered as a family to watch the *Anne of Green Gables* (1985) and *Anne of Green Gables: The Sequel* (1987) miniseries. They are a lively retelling of L. M. Montgomery's tales about the mischievous, imaginative Anne Shirley and her life growing up as an adopted orphan on Prince Edward Island in Canada. Separated into multiple episodes, the films can be spread out throughout the month.

Consider which of these or other books, television series, or films you could enjoy with your family in January.

PEOPLE PRIORITIES FOR JANUARY

When January hits, most of my (grown) kids who came home for Christmas have returned to their homes and lives, so the house is quiet. As a result, Clay and I usually have a bit of extra time to enjoy each other's company and build into each other's lives. Because January is a time for regrouping, I also make time for those friends who encourage my heart and soul.

What people do you plan to prioritize in January?
What encouraging friends will you invite to your
home or meet for a meal to start the new year off?
Make this an every-January event. I do!

_____

_____

_____

_____

_____

February

A CULTURE OF LOVE
Growing Lifelong Relationships

Love is our true destiny. We do not find the meaning of
life by ourselves alone—we find it with another.

THOMAS MERTON

Unwinding in my cozy little library, I was so engrossed in my book that I didn't even realize the sun was setting. But then I was jolted out of my reverie by the familiar sound of my cell ringtone.

"Hi, Mama!" chimed the familiar voice of one of my adult children. "I've been really busy, but I just needed to hear your voice, to know that you love me and are thinking about me. You know, there's no substitute for your words of encouragement."

I get a call like that nearly every day—and I make a few calls of my own. My children and I are a tight-knit group, joined at the hip, fast and dedicated friends. All four travel all over the world for their jobs, have their own groups of friends, and function as reasonably mature adults. And yet our friendship grows deeper and deeper through the years. Next to Clay, my children are my best friends, and we remain their dearest companions.

So it was with Jesus and His disciples. Sharing meals, walking together on dusty roads, having exuberant discussions about theology, sleeping under the stars, sharing hopes and fears, and enjoying some good laughs in between it all—this was the nature of Jesus' friendships. He wove His love and grace into the lives of all who were close to Him. And as a result they were energized, driven, and excited to spend the rest of their lives telling the world about their closest and most trusted Friend.

When the relational aspect is removed from faith, Christianity becomes a list of rules to keep, a dry obedience to abstract facts. The heart is left feeling perpetually unsatisfied. Over time, doubts and insecurities creep into our faith, and we may begin to develop guilt for not being spiritual enough. We start to hope that no one notices our failure, and—the worst consequence—we may even try to hide our dissatisfaction from God.

This is not even remotely God's will for our lives. It is a lie of the evil one whispering to us in our inadequacy. Satan wants us to live in condemnation for all the ways we are imperfect in loving. The insidious thing is that the deceptive narrative is self-perpetuating. It not only makes us believe that God just wants our obedience and good works but also makes us feel like failures when we inevitably don't live up to those standards, and this causes us to draw even further away from God.

When we observe the lives of those closest to Jesus in His earthly life—the disciples—it becomes immediately apparent that they were alive with faith and hope. Even as flawed human beings, they were filled with a power that can come only from being loved and accepted by their Savior.

This liberating love is still offered to us. God wants to be as close to us as Jesus was to His disciples and to inspire the same kindness and goodness in our hearts. If we as parents can learn to embrace our relationship with God, we will be empowered to create for our children and anyone else who crosses our doorsteps a true culture of love—a home environment where the life of God is breathed through all moments and love becomes the fuel for living with hope, purpose, and expectation.

Ultimately, God desires that we instill in the hearts of those around us the same love that has been made real in our lives. That is the crux of discipleship. Our disciples—whether they be our children, our friends, or anyone else in our care—must eventually be sent out into the world as Jesus sent out His disciples. When they have grasped the vision of the Kingdom and the King who rules it, they, too, can be world redeemers. But they need to be prepared.

Jesus knew He was sending out His disciples into a world where they would often be rejected and abused. He taught them how to handle painful encounters and asked the Father to keep them from the evil one while they were about His business. And over and over, He infused them with His love and taught them to love one another.

Our children, too, will go out into an antagonistic, difficult society. But the power that will hold them fast to the ideals they learned at home will be the bonds of love and the deep companionship we shared with them, the compassion and kindness and grace we gave to them during hard times, and the constant reassurance that they are precious to us and to God. Whatever we have spoken into the daily lives of our children is what they will hear when they are far away.

If we develop those strong bonds of love and grace, we will have the opportunity to be a continued presence in our children's lives after they do leave, to be close to them in spirit and to pursue their well-being though letters, e-mails, phone calls, and other forms of communication. I have found that I have never stopped being a mother or a discipler, no matter how old my children grow. I hope that my ongoing commitment to them through all seasons of life will inspire them to stay faithful to their calling as well.

Life in the world inevitably brings hurt, offense, and disappointment. In such circumstances love is an act of obedience, a choice to follow Christ's pattern when our natural response would be to develop bitterness or offend in return. How can children learn to make that choice unless they are taught by word and example?

I have already seen evidence that my dedication as a discipler has paid off in this area, that my children have learned to persevere in love despite the difficulties they encounter. By embracing God's love for me and then passing that love on to my children, never withholding it, I taught them how to be true lovers of people and resilient disciples themselves.

We all have such capacity to bring a spirit of grace and beauty into the world if we focus on the Lord Jesus, live in His love, and reflect that gracious love in our homes and our relationships. Our motivation comes from submitting ourselves as disciples of the One who is love Himself, who transmits committed love to us through the incredible example of His life.

My life as a disciple of Jesus hasn't always been a smooth journey. I have tested Him, misbehaved, thrown tantrums, and pulled away at times. Still He loves me. He died for me while I was yet a sinner, and He continues to extend grace to me no matter how often I stumble.

How well you love and how effectively you practice the sacrificial love of Christ in your home will determine the influence you have in the lives of others. Love is the foundation that builds bridges of understanding, insight, and willingness in others to embrace His love. We teach others how to love by showing them what it's like to receive it from a real, live, in-the-flesh person.

Ultimately, it comes down to being so transformed by Christ's love for us that we are willing to give anything to offer that love to others.

How are you doing in the love department? Are there areas where you know you're still striving against laying down your life? Ask the Lord for help. He is ready to grant it. He wants to show you what it is like to receive the unconditional love of a dedicated Parent so that you can go and do likewise, transforming your family life into a true culture of love.

At Home in the Word

1. *"Be completely humble and gentle; be patient, bearing with one another in love. Make every effort to keep the unity of the Spirit through the bond of peace" (Ephesians 4:2-3, NIV).*

   a. Children flourish when they are treated with gentleness, when loving words bring water to their souls, when affirmation is planted in their hearts. Maintaining a home atmosphere that reflects the "unity of the Spirit" requires a lot of humility and patience on the part of the parent. What are some ways you can cultivate these qualities in yourself so as to touch your children's hearts with God's unconditional love?

   b. What burdens are you carrying right now for which you would welcome love or help from others? Have you asked for this help? Why or why not?

2. *"There is one who speaks rashly like the thrusts of a sword, but the tongue of the wise brings healing" (Proverbs 12:18).*

   a. What negative words and phrases have become habitual to you? Are any of them cutting or harsh? (If you're brave enough, ask your family about this!) List some words or habitual responses you want to eliminate from your vocabulary in your family. If possible, write out a strategy for doing this.

b. Are there words and phrases of kindness that you can integrate into your home? List three kind statements you want to make instinctive in your conversations with your family (for example, "You are precious to me" or "I am so grateful for you"). Plan a strategy for creating this habit.

3. *"Above all, keep fervent in your love for one another, because love covers a multitude of sins" (1 Peter 4:8).*

a. Who in your life has wronged you—a spouse, a child, a friend or family member? Is resentment or anger qualifying your love for that person (or persons)? Write down one or two steps you could take right now to resolve the issue and restore a loving relationship. (Note: In cases of deep betrayal or abuse, restoration will not be simple and may not always be advisable. In such cases I would recommend seeking professional counseling.)

   b. What is the difference between "covering" sins with love and covering up or ignoring sins and difficulties in a family? How do you maintain an atmosphere of forgiveness, unmerited kindness, and patience without sacrificing truth?

4. *"Greater love has no one than this, that one lay down his life for his friends" (John 15:13).*

   a. Make a list of those you consider your friends in the context of this verse—loved ones for whom you would lay down your life (husband? children? other family? neighbors?). Are there people you have not included on that list to whom you can show sacrificial love? Who are these people, and how can you include them in your culture of love?

   b. What does it mean to you personally to lay down your life for those around you right now? List three ways you can show or are showing sacrificial love in your life.

Bringing It Home

What Is Your Biggest Challenge for February?

Our national ministry conferences are usually in full whirl during February, and when my kids were still at home I often struggled to juggle child care with my preparations to travel and speak. I never wanted my children to feel shortchanged, so I made sure to put aside thirty minutes or an hour daily with each child to listen and respond to his or her needs on an individual basis.

> *What do you struggle with in February?*
> *What are you doing (or could you do)*
> *to overcome that struggle?*

_____

_____

_____

_____

_____

February Anniversaries, Birthdays, and Holidays

Valentine's Day has always been a joyful time in our home. Even now I make a big breakfast for whoever happens to be at home on February 14. Chocolate chip pancakes are always on the menu, and I scatter assorted candy on each family member's place mat. I also supply cards so that we can write love notes to other family members expressing our love and gratitude.

List your own family events for February:

_____

_____

_____

_____

_____

To Read or Watch in February

Picture Books: One of our family's favorite picture books is Robert Munsch's *Love You Forever* (1986), a sweet, touching story with an easy poem to memorize. Another classic picture book is *My Mama Had a Dancing Heart* (1995), by Libba Moore Gray, with wonderful illustrations by Raúl Colón.

Literature and Nonfiction: I have always adored Catherine Marshall's *Christy* (1967), an engrossing fact-based novel about a young woman's journey as a missionary and a teacher in a rural Appalachian community in the early part of the twentieth century. In the same vein, Elisabeth Elliot's biography of Amy Carmichael, *A Chance to Die* (2005, originally published 1987), outlines that remarkable woman's experience in India as a missionary around the turn of the twentieth century.

Movies and Series: The girls in our family especially enjoy the opportunity to focus on romantic stories and films in February. *Ever After* (1998) is one of these—a charming and winsome version of the Cinderella tale set in Renaissance France and including an appearance by a very feisty Leonardo da Vinci. For you British series lovers, *Wives and Daughters* (1999) tells the story of the daughter of a country doctor in 1840s England and her interactions with her nosy neighbors. Jane Austen's novel *Emma* is also a beloved story for our family, and we particularly like the BBC miniseries adaptation with Romola Garai in the title role (2009).

Consider which of these or other books, television series, or films you could enjoy with your family in February.

People Priorities for February

For all of the people I care about, this "month of love" gives me a perfect opportunity to express my gratitude and appreciation in writing. So many people show me kindness and consideration throughout the year, and sometimes I just don't take the time to thank them. So in February I try to do just that with a card, an e-mail, or a text message. Along with a few words of thanks, I try to include a favorite memory we share or an attribute in their lives that I love.

What people do you plan to prioritize in February?
Who could use a note of love and appreciation?

_____

_____

_____

_____

_____

March

THE ART OF THE ORDINARY
Finding Beauty in Your Own Backyard

Finally, brethren, whatsoever things are true, whatsoever things
are honest, whatsoever things are just, whatsoever things are pure,
whatsoever things are lovely, whatsoever things are of good report;
if there be any virtue, and if there be any praise, think on these things.

PHILIPPIANS 4:8, KJV

After the whirlwind of a busy conference season, which usually involves countless plane flights, hotels, and faraway cities, I find it such a relief to make that final trip back to our beautiful Colorado home, nestled in the shadow of the Rocky Mountains and surrounded on all sides by snow-laden pine trees. Relaxing by candlelight, sipping coffee, and listening to gorgeous instrumental music while sharing a dessert soufflé with my family is just the kind of rest I need after those busy winter months.

Each of us has our own puzzle of life to figure out, and we assemble the pieces with the grace God provides us in our need. My puzzle of a speaking/writing/ministry life has meant that by March each year, my body is in need of restoration and the rhythms of home. In Colorado, March still clings to the chill of winter even as signs of spring begin to emerge. The persistence of cold and gray makes it that much harder to persevere with my normal responsibilities.

That is why I almost always take a break in March. The journey of ministry and homemaking to which I have been called is a long one, and if I am to make it to the end with resilience, I have to plan for adequate rest along the way.

It also helps, I've learned, to seek out beauty, especially on those long, gray days of March. I remember once that a friend told Sarah, my oldest daughter, that her love for beauty seemed a bit frivolous. Thankfully I was able to share with her that we are all responsible to keep a light burning in our souls and that beauty is one of the most profound fuels for that fire. Creating a beautiful environment and appreciating the joyful moments in the midst of a fallen, sad world not only nurtures the light in our souls but also helps give light to others.

None of us is immune to pain and ugliness in life. Allowing ourselves to admit that truth and to recognize that our difficulties may persist for years can actually free us to be intentional about staying alive and awake to God's goodness in the midst of it all. We all have to take responsibility for replenishing our souls, and God has given beauty as a watering can to hydrate the dry and shriveled parts of our lives. Just as God incarnated Himself into the world in the person of Christ, He wants to incarnate His life into our lives every day. Beauty is one of His primary means of doing that.

How do we bring more of this incarnational beauty into our lives and find refreshment when we grow weary? I've found it helps to be with people who inspire beauty in my soul and help me become centered and feel understood. These relationships provide a kind of soul sanctuary where I can stop pretending and most fully be myself. Godly friendships can act as human "cathedrals," and when we enter into the safety of their love and support, we are enabled to worship God more fully in the beauty of His holiness.

One of the ways our family has developed such "sanctuary" relationships with one another is by being intentional about spending time together over the years. Mealtimes, daily family devotions and prayer, afternoon cups of tea or coffee, dinners shared around the table, goodnight blessings—each of these is a rhythm that creates the foundation of beauty in relationships. These rhythms have become consistent, habitual disciplines that still carry us along in different seasons of life.

Developing friendships outside our home has been a challenge for me over the years because we have moved so often and because so much of my time and energy has been focused on family and ministry. But I have learned to be deliberate about investing in friendships, seeking out a few people who seem to "get" me and intentionally cultivating a relationship with these kindred spirits. I have come to treasure these close friendships, which have helped me feel less alone during difficult seasons. Investing in them even more has been a recent goal of mine. My hope is that in ten years my close friends and I will have built even more pathways to each other's hearts and shared more memories. I think my need for such friends is just going to grow as I age.

For me, at least, investing in sanctuary relationships means making time for them. I put their names on my calendar—Clay, the children, my dearest friends—and I don't let anything interfere with these commitments. And I do my best to really "be there" during the time we spend together, to focus on the other people, to share honestly, to be a source of support and encouragement, as I hope they will be with me.

In addition to cultivating relationships, our family has discovered many other ways to refresh ourselves and find beauty in the midst of our dull or ordinary days—long walks outdoors, cozy snuggles by the fire, soothing music, fresh flowers, something fragrant and delicious in the oven. When our kids were younger, Clay and I scheduled regular date nights for ourselves, enjoying dinner out on the town while the kids settled in with a sitter for a movie night. I also scheduled one-on-one dates with each child—a shopping trip with a small budget for a purchase and a treat or a stop for pastry and conversation with me at a local coffee shop.

Early in our family life we learned to appreciate the value of an impromptu adventure. When our kids were little I often would pack them into the car and hit the road with a great audiobook. We would cruise the back roads near our home and often stop for breakfast or hot chocolate along the way. Such spur-of-the-moment excursions on ordinary days created some of our best-loved memories. The possibilities are endless. Whatever idea brings fun or happiness or a touch of beauty to a gray or ordinary day can keep us going and refuel our souls. Why not throw a tea party or luncheon for kids and moms in the middle of the week, create an Easter egg hunt in the house for kids (it doesn't actually have to be Easter!), turn off the phone and enjoy a bubble bath with music and candlelight, or split a dessert in a favorite downtown café? Even a deep breath of fresh air on the back porch can make a difference.

Whatever sounds enjoyable and within reason, I do it because I've come to appreciate God's principle of rest and refreshment. Without it, we quickly lose perspective; we do not endure well, and we have difficulty seeing God's handiwork in our lives.

There is no better time than the present—no matter the busyness surrounding us or the grinding ordinariness of life—to seek out rest, pleasure, goodness, and beauty. It's always there, wherever we happen to find ourselves, though to find it we might need to hold our expectations a little more loosely and open our eyes and hearts. If we can do that, we'll be surprised at the delight that can visit itself upon us.

Take time this week to do something unexpected that will celebrate God's goodness and bless everyone in your home. Give your body, soul, and mind a chance to rest and refuel amidst the ordinary beauty God has hidden everywhere in plain sight.

At Home in the Word

1. *"He has made everything beautiful in its time. He has also set eternity in the human heart" (Ecclesiastes 3:11, NIV).*

   a. Psalm 139:14 states clearly that each of us was "fearfully and wonderfully made" by God. How does knowing that God made us to be "wonderful" affect the way you see yourself and others around you? List some ways you can attend (or not attend) to the beautiful person God has created you to be. If there are some changes you need to make in this regard, write them down too.

   b. As God is our Creator—and the source of everything beautiful—so we have been made to be cocreators of the beautiful through His Holy Spirit. List at least three creative ways you could introduce some refreshing beauty into your life or home this month.

2. *"What will it profit a man if he gains the whole world and forfeits his soul? Or what will a man give in exchange for his soul?" (Matthew 16:26).*

   a. If your soul, as the verse implies, is the most important thing you own, what priority should it take in comparison to other elements of your life? If you can, jot down an example of a time when you forgot or laid aside that truth to achieve something you wanted. What was the result? (In my own life, neglecting to care for my soul usually results in guilt, stress, and overcommitment—taking on things I was never supposed to carry.)

b. What aspects of your current life tend to drain your soul? What are your time stealers? Write down two or three; then brainstorm some strategies for eliminating nonessentials in order to refresh and restore your soul.

3. *"Watch over your heart with all diligence, for from it flow the springs of life" (Proverbs 4:23).*

a. How would you describe the current condition of your own heart? Are you distracted and discouraged? Are you full of gratitude? Write a brief evaluation of your "heart health" and one or two actions you can take to improve it.

b. List some strategies for reaching the hearts of your children and beautifying their souls as well as your own. What has worked best for you in the past? What would you like to try?

4. *"Let your adorning be the hidden person of the heart with the imperishable beauty of a gentle and quiet spirit, which in God's sight is very precious"* (*1 Peter 3:4, ESV*).

a. Practically speaking, how does one go about "adorning" one's inner person? What specific actions can you take to influence the interior design of your soul? Write down some possibilities.

b. God considers a quiet and gentle spirit to be very precious. What aspects of your life tend to distract you from quietness and gentleness? What steps can you take to quiet your soul before God?

Bringing It Home

WHAT IS YOUR BIGGEST CHALLENGE FOR MARCH?

March is the month when my travels to speak at conferences are usually wrapping up. With the return home often comes a sense of disorder in my schedule and in my soul. My challenge in this month, therefore, is to center myself into a normal day-to-day schedule. One way I have found to do this is to limit my screen use until after breakfast. That way I will be more inclined to have a quiet time and pray, which is by far the best way to start a centered day.

> *What do you struggle with in March?*
> *What are you doing (or could you do)*
> *to overcome that struggle?*

_____

_____

_____

_____

_____

MARCH ANNIVERSARIES, BIRTHDAYS, AND HOLIDAYS

March tends to be a quiet time for us as a family. For the past few years, however, my daughter Sarah and I have taken time at the end of the conference season to refresh and relax in one of our family's favorite mountain towns—Asheville, North Carolina. We also use the time to work on our respective writing projects.

List your own family events for March:

_____

_____

_____

_____

_____

To Read or Watch in March

Picture Books: Margaret Early wrote and illustrated multiple children's books filled with stunning artwork reminiscent of stained-glass windows or medieval tapestries. Her versions of *William Tell* (1991) and *Robin Hood* (1996) are enjoyable for all ages.

Literature and Nonfiction: Madeleine L'Engle's *Walking on Water* (1980) is a reflection on how Christ beautifies our lives by helping us to recognize the incarnational in every aspect of life, from soapy dishwater to a breathtaking sunset. It is a wonderful guidebook on appreciating the art of the ordinary.

Movies and Series: We Clarksons are big Jane Austen fans; we find her witty depiction of nineteenth-century English culture delightful and engrossing. Many film adaptations have been made of her books over the years. One of our favorites is the six-part BBC miniseries of *Pride and Prejudice,* starring Colin Firth and Jennifer Ehle (1995). While the 2005 film version with Keira Knightley is also very enjoyable, we prefer the longer version because we think it recreates Austen's incisive account of character and countryside more accurately.

Consider which of these or other books, television series, or films you could enjoy with your family in March.

PEOPLE PRIORITIES FOR MARCH

My daughter Sarah is a special priority in March because of our annual trip to Asheville together. I treasure this week to focus on my firstborn, to dream with her and find refreshment from the busyness of life together. Sarah is a great lover of beauty, and being with her always reminds me of the importance of seeking out beauty anywhere we are in life.

What people do you plan to prioritize in March?
What can you do to bring beauty into someone's life?

_____

_____

_____

_____

_____

April

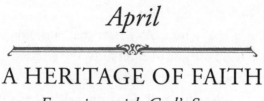

A HERITAGE OF FAITH
Engaging with God's Story

*Faith is to believe what you do not yet see; the reward
for this faith is to see what you believe.*

ST. AUGUSTINE

The house is still, my bed so cozy, and the sun's first rays are only just now reflecting on the Colorado foothills a few miles away. Even though the drowsiness of sleep lingers, already I can hear the notes of the song that calls out to me every morning. It is my wake-up call, and before I even realize it, I am quietly exiting my bed to start my morning routine.

I slide on my slippers, feel my way through the darkness to the hallway, and shuffle quietly to the kitchen, headed straight for the teakettle. It, too, is slow to get started at this early morning hour, so while I wait for the water to boil, I gaze out the window and through the pine trees to see the glow of sunlight gaining strength on the mountainside.

Tiptoeing to the library with my prepared cup of tea, I flip on the light, sink into my overstuffed chair, and bury myself in the warm, familiar blanket that remains faithfully draped over the couch during the cold winter months. Leaning over, I select several items from my book basket, including my Bible.

Everything is ready now. As I take that first nourishing sip of strong English tea, I prepare to enter into conversation, petition, and reflection with the Lord of the universe.

Spending focused time with God on a daily basis is not always easy. Some days it almost feels impossible. But I've learned that what I draw from the well of His goodness in those quiet, unseen moments will do more than just quench my need. It will also be available for me to provide for the spiritually thirsty I encounter along the way. The river of God's goodness will flow through me and nourish all who cross my path. My investment in our time together will pay off in my words, my actions, my faith, and my values.

One of my sons enjoyed reading Malcolm Gladwell's *Outliers: The Story of Success* (2008), which examines how and why certain high achievers achieve greatness. One concept that was particularly invigorating for my son was the notion that it takes around ten thousand hours of practicing a skill for one to gain expertise. After explaining the concept to me, he pondered out loud, "Mom, I bet you have spent at least ten thousand hours in the Word of God. That makes you an expert in the Bible."

"I'm not an expert by any means," I protested. Yet when we added up my probable time spent in Scripture and prayer during all those morning quiet times, even allowing for significant time off each year, we came up with a number well beyond ten thousand hours.

It didn't happen all at once, of course. I racked up those hours slowly, morning by morning. Even as a magnificent mansion is built one brick at a time, so ten thousand hours come one hour at a time. Having a morning devotional time was a practice that I was taught as a young college student. And so by the time I got married and had children, it had already become a life habit.

I still don't know if I'm a Bible expert. But I do know that those hours invested over the years have given me a constant stream of

Scripture at my command. Certain verses surprise me all the time by occurring to me at needed moments throughout the day.

The Bible is, in a sense, God's vocabulary, and the hours I have invested in studying His Word have helped me speak and think in His language. When I pray, His promises from the Bible come to mind. When I am discouraged, verses of encouragement occur to me. When I am uncertain, Scriptures of power immediately visit themselves upon me.

Throughout those years of building my foundation of Scripture, I had seasons of feeling distant from God. In other seasons my sense of devotion was practically nonexistent because of life issues that took over. But still I persisted, even in those dry seasons. And now I can look back over many decades of perseverance and know that it was all worth it. My reward is a continual fountain of Scripture that waters the garden of my soul.

You, too, can start right where you are to make a habit of investing in God and His Word. There are a number of things that will assist you in your journey:

- Gather some devotional books in a basket near a comfy chair, and you will always have a rich variety of options for spending time with God, even if you just read for a few moments at any time.
- Plan out a time that suits your season of life and your personality. Morning suits me, but midday or evening could work just as well. The important thing is that you do it.
- Consider how you could also incorporate devotional time into your family life. Pick a time—at breakfast, before school, on weekends, or before bed—to read and discuss Scripture together, and encourage your children in their own age-appropriate devotions. My adult children have often mentioned to me that hearing verses almost every day of their youth gave them their own treasure trove

of Scripture that even to this day encourages them and provides words of truth.

If you make your relationship with God a priority, you will be astonished at the harvest you will reap after many years. The kind of faith that develops through a daily investment of time is a firm rock that nothing can move.

At Home in the Word

1. *"Without faith it is impossible to please God, because anyone who comes to him must believe that he exists and that he rewards those who earnestly seek him" (Hebrews 11:6, NIV).*

    a. How specifically do you seek God? Write down several things you are currently doing—or ways you can begin to earnestly seek His presence.

    b. What helps strengthen your faith in God's existence and His goodness? This can be anything from listening to music to walking in nature to talking with other people who believe—or something else entirely. (Having a handful of godly friends who encourage me in my faith has helped me immensely during dark, doubtful times, and keeping a gratitude journal helps me remember the ways He has worked faithfully in my life.) List several of these practices that you want to incorporate more fully into your daily life.

2. *"Truly I say to you, if you have faith the size of a mustard seed, you will say to this mountain, 'Move from here to there,' and it will move; and nothing will be impossible to you" (Matthew 17:20).*

   a. Make a list of the "mountains" or obstacles that are looming ahead in your life. Are you leaning on your own abilities to address these issues or on God's capability to take whatever trust you can muster and do good with it? Does trusting in God mean you should be completely passive and not take any action to address the obstacle—or can faith work together with action?

   b. Is there anything that you and your family need to pray together about? Scripture says that "a cord of three strands is not quickly broken" (Ecclesiastes 4:12, NIV). Make a list of items to bring to your family prayer times.

3. *"We walk by faith, not by sight" (2 Corinthians 5:7).*

   a. What does it mean to walk by faith when you cannot see or understand the next step? If possible, write down an example of this from your own experience or the experience of someone you know.

b. Are there circumstances in your life right now that you simply cannot understand or cannot see God working in? Make a list of those circumstances. Next to each one write, "I give this to God, who sees what I cannot see."

4. *"My message and my preaching were not with wise and persuasive words, but with a demonstration of the Spirit's power, so that your faith might not rest on human wisdom, but on God's power"* (*1 Corinthians 2:4-5, NIV*).

a. What do you tend to lean on *first* when approaching problems and difficulties—human wisdom or God's power? If we're honest, most of us tend to rely on human wisdom first and only turn to God later when our human wisdom fails. What can you do to increase your tendency to turn to God first? Do you think there is ever a place for human wisdom in decision making? Why or why not?

b. Are there problems in your family—a wayward child, a difficult financial situation—that feel beyond you? Make a list of the issues that are troubling you now and commit each one to prayer. Write out your prayer or just jot down a summary of the issues you prayed about; then place them all into the file drawers of heaven and watch God work.

Bringing It Home

WHAT IS YOUR BIGGEST CHALLENGE FOR APRIL?

With all the snow that Colorado winters bring, by April I usually have a serious case of cabin fever. So this is a favored month to get outdoors, delight in the beauty of the impending spring, and start planting flowers. Visiting a garden shop or greenhouse always fills me with pleasure.

What do you struggle with in April? What are you doing (or could you do) to overcome that struggle?

_____

_____

_____

_____

_____

APRIL ANNIVERSARIES, BIRTHDAYS, AND HOLIDAYS

Holy Week and Easter, which often fall in April, are deeply meaningful events for our family. As described in *The Lifegiving Home*, we participate in a variety of services during the week before Easter, remembering the events leading up to Jesus' crucifixion. Our observance culminates in a joyful celebration of the Feast of the Resurrection followed by an Easter feast at home and a gigantic Easter egg hunt that includes adults as well as children. I buy as many colors and sizes of plastic eggs as I can find and fill them with a variety of treats. Each person gets his or her own size or color. I've found that great memories are made when fun is celebrated generationally.

List your own family events for April:

_____

_____

_____

_____

_____

To Read or Watch in April

Picture Books: Margaret Hodges's *Saint George and the Dragon* (1984), with its exquisite hand-drawn illustrations by Trina Schart Hyman, was one of our favorite picture books. With the traditional Feast of St. George happening annually on April 23, this Caldecott award winner could be a great accompaniment to discovering the true story of a hero of the church.

Literature and Nonfiction: Elizabeth Goudge was a scholar's daughter who spent her early years in England's cathedral towns. Her novels and short stories were bestsellers from the 1930s until the 1970s and are still widely read today. Beloved by several Clarksons, they are not to be missed. (My Sarah recommends *Pilgrim's Inn*, 1948, as a good place to start.)

Movies and Series: Eric Liddell, who won a gold medal for the four-hundred-meter race at the 1924 Olympics and went on to become a missionary in China, was brilliantly immortalized in the biopic *Chariots of Fire* (1981). An inspiring story of dedicated faith, it contrasts Liddell's approach to life with that of Harold Abrahams, a fellow Olympic team member. It is an inspiring true story that the whole family can enjoy.

Consider which of these or other books, television series, or films you could enjoy with your family in April.

PEOPLE PRIORITIES FOR APRIL

My younger son, Nathan, is always a priority for us in April because his birthday falls in this month. I love to celebrate him and the way he is growing in life. During the week of his birthday, I spend a portion of each day praying especially for his needs. (I do this for each of my children's birthdays.)

This month of Holy Week and Easter is also a time when I love to focus on my family in Christ—my fellow believers, especially those I worship with regularly. How grateful I am for other believers to love me, challenge me, pray for me, and encourage me.

What people do you plan to prioritize in April? What brothers and sisters in Christ can you love and celebrate?

_____

_____

_____

_____

_____

May

DAYS TO COMMEMORATE
Marking Growth with Celebration

The master said, "Well done, my good and faithful servant.
You have been faithful in handling this small amount, so now I will
give you many more responsibilities. Let's celebrate together!"

MATTHEW 25:23, NLT

May is an important time for celebrating accomplishments—graduations, music recitals, sports competitions. But I want to especially highlight motherhood here because May is also the month we celebrate motherhood—and mothers matter!

Culture has lost imagination for how important a mother's role truly is, and yet even in this brave new world we live in, it is no less true that, as William Ross Wallace wrote in 1865, "the hand that rocks the cradle is the hand that rules the world." When we understand that a mother's influence will shape the minds, hearts, values, souls, and faith of the next generation, we will celebrate her role indeed.

Instead of sharing from my experience as a mother, I give you my daughter Sarah. Her words on a recent Mother's Day spoke so dearly and deeply to me.

Dear Mom,

We just don't seem able to manage a Mother's Day together, do we? Well, in your absence and decidedly in your honor, I have a story to tell. Perhaps you'll think it an odd one for a tribute to your motherhood. A workaday tale it may be, but in my mind it is a bright, unfading gem. For what you gave me one Texas morning almost twenty years ago remains a grace that forms the bedrock of my heart. Memories don't get much better than that, odd or not. Here goes.

I stood with munchkin nose pressed hard against the back door glass. Outside the skies tumbled and fought, the rain fell in torrents for the fifth day in a row, and the roar of newborn creeks called me even through the panes. Behind me you gathered books and pencils for a morning of homeschool, switching on the lamps to battle the outdoor gloom. But even as you did, the boys slipped beside me, glued their noses to the window too, and when you called us we turned three small, grieved faces away from a world that seemed tailor made for splashing and exploration.

"Aw, Mom," we groaned, timid but yearning for that alluring realm beyond. "Can't we just go outside and explore today?"

I still remember how startled I was at your yes. The way you were silent for a second, took a deep breath, pushed the books aside, and put your hands on your hips.

"Old shoes and old clothes on before you go," you ordered, and we hastened for our gear, grabbing boots and jackets, hearts pattering in elation at this wholly unexpected day. We were back in two minutes, and behold, so were you. A tiny jolt touched my heart at the sight of you decked in scuffed shoes and old jeans, intent upon joining our expedition. I hadn't expected that the queen would lead the adventure.

You were, of course, the same queen who would also wash
the several loads of muddy clothes resulting from it, mop up our
boot prints on the kitchen floor, and defend our bedraggled state
to my grandmother when we returned. (It was her house, after
all.) But I was too little to know all of that. All I knew was
that your presence hallowed the adventure. And ah, there was so
much we longed to show you.

Out we tromped into a world all awhisper, the air tingling
with the rain, the sky swift and changeful as the rivulets below.
In an ecstasy of abandon we jumped in every puddle to be found
within the first ten feet, twirled and whooped and ran all out,
limbs loose and swinging, to the pasture gate that led to the
tank—the pond, where the cattle watered. There the real drama
awaited—a real flood down by the giant oak, now up to his
waist in new-made rivers.

"Come on, Mom!" we screeched above the roar of the
water, picking our way through the mud of the old cattle
trails, ducking beneath cedar branches and wintered vines.
You came. Smiling, eyebrows arched in interest at every
fossil we pointed out, every yell of false alarm when a branch
turned out not to be a snake. You came right into the streams,
splashed us with the cold, swift water, and when we eyed the
swiftest torrent with daring, hungry eyes, you nodded your
permission. In we went, right up to our short little waists,
fighting against the current in an overjoyed grapple with the
one joyous fact of the water.

I remember that for one instant I looked back at you.
Already in the current, I turned and sought your face. I was a
little in awe that you would let us dare the flood. I was proud
that you were there to see us do it. And if I was also a little
afraid of the torrent, well, I had you at my back. You caught my
eye. And to this day I cannot forget the glint of fun that blazed

*in your glance. The slight nod of reassurance that told me I
would never be out of your sight. Then the smile, like a whisper
between those who know the great camaraderie of adventure.
I laughed. And dove straight in.*

*And that, Mom, is one of the clarion moments for which
I will thank you all my days.*

*For in that instant you gave me your own heroic view of life.
I know now that courage was always your mark. You were a
dreamer, a lover of the underdog, a missionary in Communist
Poland, a writer, a teacher, daring in faith and fierce in
friendship. And even when three squirmy children invaded your
life (four, eventually, with Joy), you kept that courage strong.
You brought it right into your motherhood and determined that
we should learn it too.*

*That rainy-day adventure was a lesson in valor, in gladness,
in dreams. You wanted your children to taste the haunting grace
of the world, so you freed us to heed the cry of the rain. You
knew that danger is always close, so you came too. You knew
that life is full of risk, so when we met the dare of the water, you
let us hope and reach and try, and you taught us the boldness
with which this thing called life must be met.*

*Only now, grown up as I am, with the demons of oughts
and shoulds ever breathing down my neck, do I understand
the import of the choice you made that morning. You could
have said no. You could have resolutely shut that door, glared
down our yearning little hearts, rebuked our impractical
imaginations. You could have insisted on an ordinary day
and a checklist of chores.*

*But you saw that our hearts were ripe for the forming. You
saw that holy hunger for far horizons. You saw our need to try,
to dare, to reach for something just beyond our grasp. So you
opened the door. Be bold, said your eyes. Be joyous. Be brave
with my blessing.*

But you also gave us yourself. Your presence was the strength at our back, your laughter the song that sent us leaping through the rain. You stood there on the creek bank, eagle-eyed, cheerful, strong, and the sight of you glimpsed through the splash and rain sent a courage like blood pulsing through our veins. We tried all the harder because you were there. We dared because we knew you would await us at the end. And when we tromped home, gloriously wet and utterly exhausted, it was you who sat us by the fire, brewed the cocoa, and lingered with us in the flickering light. Your interest made us heroes. We told of the current that nearly got us, the branch that nearly broke, the newest fossil found, and it was your admiring words that turned us into knights at battle's end, triumphant and ready to fight again.

To know that life is a great quest is one thing. To be given the love to meet it is another altogether. You, my precious mother, gave us both.

Courage in living and love that does not fail—these themes defined my childhood. That one bright day was a note in a larger song. When life was dark, you lit candles. When times were grim, you made a feast (even if it was only homemade bread and cheese). When the battle I faced was doubt of God, you looked me in the eye and said, "He's bigger than your doubts." But then you took my hand: "Don't worry. I'll have faith for you until yours lives again."

When sickness came, when friendships failed, you challenged me to write, to love, to hope with every fiber of my being. When Oxford seemed a dream beyond all grasping, you said, "Just try." And when, once there, I thought for sure my essays would be flops, you ordered me to take a good long walk, drink tea, and "give it one more go."

Meet the battle and face it with a song. Light a candle and lay a feast in the very teeth of darkness. Dare, always, to try once more. To love again. That's what you taught me.

So here's to you, beloved and valiant mother o' my heart. You make me think of Tennyson's lines in "Ulysses":

That which we are, we are;
One equal temper of heroic hearts.

To have shared your heart and learned your courage is a gift that will follow me all my days. I hope I learn to be as brave as you.

Happy Mother's Day.
Love, Sarah

At Home in the Word

1. *"Remember the sabbath day, to keep it holy" (Exodus 20:8).*

   a. God told the Israelites to remember the Sabbath day. To remember something, it must be kept fresh in the mind and practiced regularly. What additional rhythms (special days, holidays) do you observe with your family on a regular basis—daily, weekly, monthly, or yearly? Write down at least three.

   b. Why do you think God made the Sabbath? What is your personal experience of keeping the Sabbath? What would you like it to be?

2. *"Behold, children are a gift of the LORD, the fruit of the womb is a reward" (Psalm 127:3).*

    a. Most parents need this reminder from time to time because parenting is hard work, and it's easy to fall into the habit of thinking of our children as a challenge and a distraction. How can thinking of your children as a reward and an opportunity change the way you treat them? What can you do to remind yourself of this truth when you forget?

    b. Have you ever considered that your children are not only a gift to you but a gift to others as well? They will carry on your heritage and, hopefully, carry God's grace into a needy world. In what ways can you encourage your children to consider their stewardship in the world? How can you encourage their particular talents and gifts? Write down at least three ideas.

3. *"You shall have the fiftieth year as a jubilee; you shall not sow, nor reap its aftergrowth, nor gather in from its untrimmed vines. For it is a jubilee; it shall be holy to you" (Leviticus 25:11-12).*

    a. In this busy modern era, it is so easy to give short shrift to special days and special events. What do you think would happen if we treated birthdays, holidays, rites of passage, and other such events in our lives with the same respect that the Israelites gave to the Year of Jubilee? What special family days would you like to treat more seriously, and how could you do this?

b. We live in a casual age, when the use of special clothes, special objects, and physical rituals to show honor and reverence and to recognize solemn events has largely been set aside. As a result, I fear, we have only a limited vocabulary for honoring what is truly special. What are some specific ways you can mark what is special and sacred in your home and model honor and reverence for your children? (This could involve anything from using special dishes to kneeling for prayer.)

4. *"Blessed are those who are invited to the marriage supper of the Lamb" (Revelation 19:9).*

a. What is the difference between a feast and an ordinary meal? What do you think is the special significance of celebrating the end of time with a banquet—and what does that tell us about how we are to live in the meantime?

b. Do you practice feasting with your family? This could be literal—joyful meals with delicious food in abundance—or more figurative—feasting on the beauty of nature, or an exciting conversation. Write down several different ways you can practice "feasting" with your family. Add a short list of people you can invite to share your feasting. Then make a plan to implement one of your ideas this week.

Bringing It Home

WHAT IS YOUR BIGGEST CHALLENGE FOR MAY?

When my kids were still at home, I tended to dread the end of May, when the regularity and reliability of the school year inevitably gave way to endless hours with four rambunctious kids, all with different expectations. I learned to prepare myself so that when the summer break arrived, I would accept the season for what it was and not try to overschedule or control the days. The result was that I often enjoyed making wonderful memories with my kids and husband that otherwise wouldn't have happened.

What do you struggle with in May? What are you doing
(or could you do) to overcome that struggle?

_____

_____

_____

_____

May Anniversaries, Birthdays, and Holidays

May is undeniably the month of commemoration and celebration for us Clarksons. With three family birthdays (Joy, Clay, and Sarah) and Mother's Day to boot, it can feel like a nonstop party, with gift giving, flurries of greeting cards, and all-you-can-eat cinnamon rolls and scrambled eggs (our favorite go-to birthday breakfast). We have learned to enjoy and relish the memories in the midst of the whirlwind of it all.

List your own family events for May:

_____

_____

_____

_____

_____

To Read or Watch in May

Picture Books: Beatrix Potter is one of the most beloved children's book authors, with her charmingly illustrated tales of animals in the English countryside—*The Tale of Peter Rabbit* (1902) was her first and arguably her most famous. Jill Barklem's quaint Brambly Hedge books (1980–2010) are in a similar vein.

Literature and Nonfiction: Gene Stratton-Porter, a naturalist and writer at the turn of the twentieth century, authored *Freckles* (1904) and *A Girl of the Limberlost* (1909) about her early life near the long-gone Limberlost swamp in eastern Indiana. Later she moved to California, which inspired her redemptive novel, *The Keeper of the Bees* (1925).

Movies and Series: In the past couple of decades, the Pixar and DreamWorks studios have each released a stream of wonderful digitally animated films that our family has really enjoyed. Some of our favorites include *How to Train Your Dragon* (2010), *The Incredibles* (2004), and *Finding Nemo* (2003). Though we weren't big fans of the first *Toy Story* (1995)—too dark for some of my children's tastes—we loved the second and third films in the series.

Consider which of these or other books, television series, or films you could enjoy with your family in May.

PEOPLE PRIORITIES FOR MAY

Joy is my youngest, my precious "bonus" from God in my early forties. She is also a songbird and keeps great song playlists on her phone. A few years ago, she and I started going for late Sunday afternoon drives on the quiet back roads near our home. We play her music loudly and breathe in the beauty of the Rocky Mountain foothills. It's one of my favorite things to do, even in the middle of a busy month. She is an important priority for me in May, her birthday month.

> *What people do you plan to prioritize in May? If you're a mother, this is the perfect time to make yourself a priority for once. Why not plan something to comfort and refresh your soul and body—a new outfit, a special lunch with a friend, or just some quiet time alone in a beautiful place?*

_____

_____

_____

_____

June

TIMES OF DELIGHT
Creating a Value for Play

You can discover more about a person in an hour
of play than in a year of conversation.
ATTRIBUTED TO PLATO

The memory of camping out on our deck under an endless expanse of twinkling stars, aspen leaves shivering and whispering in the mountain breeze, staring into the vast canopy of space and squinting to see a fleeting shooting star, is still as vivid to me now as it was when our family experienced it so many years ago. Even in the midst of the overwhelming, nonstop craziness of our family life, those nights of sleeping out under the stars were transformative. The simple act of going outside and enjoying nature changed the entire tone of our life together.

In the bustle of a busy household, especially when people are overworked and tired, tempers tend to flare and unkind words are spoken. It happens to everyone, and it certainly happened to us—often. In my urge to get things done, I would turn into a drill sergeant and the rest of the family, depending on their personalities, would rebel or turn sullen or simply disappear.

At such times, what we all needed was a vacation—time to rest, play, and escape the machine of busyness for a time. A vacation wasn't always feasible, but we found that camping at home could be just the ticket to ease our stress and cool our irritations.

The night would invariably begin with pizza and root beer floats for the kids. We would take our meal outside and enjoy it in the cool, refreshing mountain air. Once done with dinner, the kids would take to our expansive yard, running wildly around playing flashlight tag as dusk descended. I would watch from the second-story deck with Clay, gazing out toward Colorado Springs. Our house at the time sat on a long ridge nestled up against the foothills of the Rockies, more than a thousand feet higher than most of the population in the city. So when I looked out, I could see the whole metropolis spanning before me, the infinite lights sparkling below. Even after a few short minutes, I could feel myself relaxing, my spirit growing quieter.

(It was on one of these amazing evenings when four-year-old Joy said, "Mama, wif all dese lights in de sky sparkling, evewybody can see Jesus is a good Artist.")

My life in those days was hyperfocused on the mundane challenges in my immediate line of sight. But God wanted to show me that there was so much more of beauty, light, and life to be experienced just inches above the surface of my hectic life. I could not perceive it because the false lights of the world and the noisy voices of others had drowned out the beauty God meant for me. But He patiently waited for me with a world of beauty prepared to overwhelm my senses and transform my perspective.

Do you remember the story of Jesus' friend Mary, who loved to hang out with her Lord, and of her hardworking sister Martha, who bitterly resented it? Martha complained, "Lord, do You not care that my sister has left me to do all the serving alone?" (Luke 10:40).

Jesus immediately understood what Martha needed most—and it wasn't help with the housework! He answered her, "Martha, Martha, you are worried and bothered about so many things; but only one thing is necessary, for Mary has chosen the good part, which shall not be taken away from her" (verses 41-42).

I have spent far too much of my life in Martha's place of workaholic anxiety, lost in the maze of my worries. I always intend to enjoy each day, to enjoy time with my husband and children, to memorize the golden moments that make the love in our home so special to my heart. But all too often I have just kept on trudging forward, obsessed with getting things done. By the time I begin to question whether I have truly captured the essence of God's presence in a given day, I have already lost what could have been the joy of the Spirit moving in my life. How easy it is for me to focus on the to-do list and to miss what could be experienced and enjoyed.

As I grow older I am increasingly made aware that life flies by at a stunning pace. And I have come to believe with all my heart that, in the end, how I love and how I am loved in return will matter far more than what I accomplish. But it's one thing to believe that truth and something else entirely to live it.

I will freely tell you that loving my children and husband has often required me to sacrifice my own goals and desires, my plans and expectations. So often I have had to throw my schedule out the window in order to listen, to be a friend, to share mutual joys, to cry with those I care about and play with them too. Taking time to love well usually requires choosing a simpler life that has the flexibility to cultivate friendships in unexpected moments.

It took me a long time to realize this—that my busyness, my heavy workload, my lofty goals and ideals were actually getting in the way of that kind of life. That something had to change—something had to go.

Most of us these days are overstimulated, transfixed by our phones, computers, and social media. We have a million appointments and barely manage to fit our daily Starbucks into the margins. Our modern culture considers it normal to stuff as many activities as possible into our days, to juggle a million demands and possibilities. Then, when we inevitably drop one of them, we feel defeated.

If we want to live truly meaningful, fruitful lives, it is absolutely crucial that we buck this trend—that we learn to breathe, relax, focus on what really matters. The dishes might wait an hour, but a lonely child may not. A phone call can be rescheduled; a moment of shared laughter may never come again.

So we must ask ourselves: Do the priority people in our lives (spouse, children, close friends) feel we are often distracted by all the things we do? Do they comment on how much they appreciate our ability to give full attention to them, or do they complain that we never listen or have time for them? Can we possibly give unconditional love to our family and create an atmosphere of grace in our homes if we are driving ourselves unmercifully? Are we taking care of our souls or setting unattainable and unrealistic goals for our lives and feeling like a failure when we fail to meet them?

Busyness doesn't just mean neglecting our children, our spouses, or even ourselves; ultimately it means neglecting our heavenly Father as well. He is so ready to grant us peace and to guide us in wisdom through His gentle voice. But He desires our presence, and when we keep our focus on what we are determined to accomplish, we put barriers up in front of God. We create our own conundrums by refusing to take time to be comforted in the presence of our living, loving Father.

Psalm 90:10, 12 gives us a healthy reminder of what is important in life:

As for the days of our life, they contain seventy years,
Or if due to strength, eighty years,
Yet . . . soon it is gone and we fly away. . . .
So teach us to number our days,
That we might present to You a heart of wisdom.

In light of this biblical advice, doesn't it make sense to think about and adjust our lives and schedules? What activities and obligations need to go? What needs to be added to ensure that you and your family experience more love, more peace, more fun and affection?

We each have a choice, every day of our lives. Will we take time to celebrate the joys that God has provided, the beauty that He wants us to explore? Will we experience the sweetness of intimacy that comes from investing heart time with those we love? Will we take time to experience the pleasures God provides us so generously, to "taste and see that the LORD is good" (Psalm 34:8)? The chores and responsibilities will always be there, but the time to invest in the ones we love, to look them in the eye, to give an unexpected kiss on the cheek, to laugh at the craziness of moments and let loose with joyful, uninhibited play—that time will pass in the blink of an eye.

Today, I urge both you and myself to take full advantage of the moments of our lives. Accept them as the gifts they are and celebrate them fully. Breathe deep. Listen well. Laugh easily. Have fun with those you love. And don't forget the hugs and kisses.

At Home in the Word

1. "He called a child to Himself and set him before [His disciples], and said, 'Truly I say to you, unless you are converted and become like children, you will not enter the kingdom of heaven'" (Matthew 18:2-3).

    a. Why do we need to become like children to enter the Kingdom of Heaven? What characteristics do children have that merit them such an honor? (If it helps, look at the lives of your own children and the ways in which they might exemplify Kingdom life.)

b. What can you learn from your children about what it means to be Christlike? List three childlike qualities you would like for yourself.

2. *"David was dancing before the LORD with all his might"*
   (2 Samuel 6:14).

   a. What do you do to "dance" with God—what fills your heart with joy? Write out how you feel about taking time to enjoy life while putting away constant busyness. Do you ever feel you should always be working or getting something done?

   b. Dancing enthusiastically before the Lord can be an act of worship. So can kneeling in a quiet church, volunteering in a soup kitchen, or taking a brisk walk outdoors. What do all these forms of worship have in common? (What makes them worship?) Given your personality and beliefs, what acts of worship help you feel closest to God?

JUNE: TIMES OF DELIGHT || 59

3. *"How precious is Your lovingkindness, O God! . . . The children of men . . . drink their fill of the abundance of Your house; and You give them to drink of the river of Your delights. For with You is the fountain of life; in Your light we see light" (Psalm 36:7-9).*

a. What are the signs in your household that you have become too busy or that you need a fresh perspective—to "see light"? List three typical "symptoms" you can watch for (like, for instance, my "drill sergeant" tendencies).

b. What kinds of experiences help you and your family relax, enjoy one another, gain fresh perspective, and taste God's goodness ("the river of . . . delights")? List at least three— anything from a hot bath to a nature walk to an overseas vacation. What would it take to enjoy one of these activities within the next week? (If thinking this way triggers that "I just don't have time" reflex—that may be a signal that you really need to make the time!)

c. What current activities or involvements could you sacrifice to make more room for healing downtime in your life? Write down at least two possibilities and notice how you feel about giving them up (relief, anxiety, something else?).

4. *"There is nothing better for a man than to eat and drink and tell himself that his labor is good. This also I have seen that it is from the hand of God" (Ecclesiastes 2:24).*

   a. In the end, love and relationship will matter more than our accomplishments. But that doesn't mean our work is unimportant or meaningless. Take a minute to list three to five of the most important work commitments in your life. (Unpaid work counts. So does otherwise dull work done to support your family.) Why do you believe these tasks matter?

   b. God has given good life—both work and play—to you as a gift. What practical steps can you take to find a healthy balance between the two?

Bringing It Home

WHAT IS YOUR BIGGEST CHALLENGE FOR JUNE?

June is usually when I started to run out of steam. The school year, the impending heat and humidity of summer, and the craziness of everyone running around the house instead of being focused on studies just about did me in. So I learned early on to involve each of my kids in a library reading program. This gave them a way to be active and out of the house through the summer. Swimming lessons were also immensely helpful.

*What do you struggle with in June? What are you doing
(or could you do) to overcome that struggle?*

_____

_____

_____

_____

_____

June Anniversaries, Birthdays, and Holidays

In recent years I have hosted many leadership retreats for the women
who work with me in my ministry. June is the perfect time of year
for such an event. The heat of summer hasn't quite taken hold, and
yet everything is verdant and beautiful. I fill my rooms with flowers
and place pots and pots of flowers out on our front porch and back
deck. We feel like we're meeting in a garden!

List your own family events for June:

_____

_____

_____

_____

_____

To Read or Watch in June

Picture Books: C. W. Anderson's Billy and Blaze series (written between 1936 and 1969) is a collection of delightfully illustrated short books about a boy who receives a pony for his birthday and their adventures together. My boys especially loved to hear these read out loud when they were little.

Literature and Nonfiction: The turn of the twentieth century saw the creation of many wonderful books for youth. In the US, Frances Hodgson Burnett wrote timeless novels like *Little Lord Fauntleroy* (1885–1886) and *The Secret Garden* (1911), while Eleanor Porter penned heartwarming stories about small-town America like *Pollyanna* (1913) and *Just David* (1916). (Our family loves *Just David* so much that we arranged to put it back in print for our audiences.) Meanwhile, on the other side of the Atlantic, readers were enjoying the Johanna Spyri's Swiss classic, *Heidi* (1881); E. Nesbit was writing such English treasures as *The Railway Children* (1906) and *The Story of the Treasure Seekers* (1899); and Kenneth Grahame was authoring his whimsical animal adventure tale, *The Wind in the Willows* (1908). Though these books were aimed toward a young audience, readers of any age could enjoy them—and still do. They are definitely some of my favorite read-alouds.

Movies and Series: The BBC is a wonderful resource for film adaptations of many of the aforementioned books. Standouts are *The Wind in the Willows* (2006), *The Railway Children* (1968), and *Pollyanna* (1973).

Consider which of these or other books, television series, or films you could enjoy with your family in June.

PEOPLE PRIORITIES FOR JUNE

Because I usually host my dear friends and partners in ministry for our retreat weekend in June, this is the month I make them a priority.

I also like to celebrate the children in my life in this first month of summer vacation. When my kids were home, I often had each one invite a friend over to share breakfast on our porch. I would serve cheesy eggs, fruit, and toast, then send them all out to play. These days I am more likely to invite some young mothers along with their children. The mothers love the fellowship and support, and the children love playing with one another in our yard.

What people do you plan to prioritize in June?
How can you build more joyful relationships
with the children in your life?

_____

_____

_____

_____

_____

July

A HEROIC HERITAGE
Engaging with Story and History

[God] gives wisdom to wise men
And knowledge to men of understanding.

DANIEL 2:21

The eleventh chapter of Hebrews pays tribute to men and women—Abel, Abraham, Sarah, David, and many others—who lived in the warp and woof of life's trials but, instead of giving in to the cultural norms of compromise, kept their eyes on heaven and lived exceptional lives. They made decisions to trust God in all the hard places, and as a result "God is not ashamed to be called their God" (verse 16).

These are people who made the story of the Bible worth knowing, the men and women who set a pattern for us to follow. They are our spiritual heroes—and we are called to follow in their footsteps.

We hear a lot about heroes these days, mostly in terms of specific acts of physical or emotional bravery. We celebrate soldiers and firefighters and get excited about civilians who pull strangers from burning vehicles. We love to watch movies about "good guys" fighting "forces of evil" on a grand scale and superheroes with special powers. Such tales of heroism can be entertaining and even inspiring. But they often give a limited and skewed picture of what it really means to be a hero.

True heroism starts with a passion to love and serve God through actions, stewardship, relationships, and obedience. True heroes are in the habit of serving others because they are compelled to give as Jesus gave. They are motivated to endure and do good not only in big, climactic battles but also in the grind of everyday living. And when a sacrifice is required, when the need to lay down one's life for another comes along, true heroes are not surprised; they have already been imagining this to be their service of worship to God.

Sadly, I fear, our culture is deficient in that kind of hero. I recently found myself in a meeting with a group of high-level business leaders. The conversation centered on new recruits from universities, many of whom were already in a position to make important decisions. I can still remember an elderly executive, an advisor for and recruiter of many of these newest team members, who shared his unvarnished thoughts.

The problem, he said, was that most younger college graduates who were applying for these positions were ill prepared to take on such responsibility. "They have not read broadly on many subjects and haven't developed a strong worldview. As a consequence, they have almost no historical perspective.

"Because they are media dependent," he added, these kids "are subject to believing popular views espoused by that media. Because they have been raised on quick sound bites and insubstantial TV 'wisdom,' their opinions are shallow and reactionary. Thinking clearly, synthesizing high-minded ideas, developing an appetite for substantial literature, immersing themselves in the works of great, classical thinkers—not only are these things not part of their daily habits; they are as good as alien to them. Add to that a lack of character training and an inability to do hard work through difficult seasons, and you will find it almost impossible to find an excellent candidate who can handle such important responsibilities."

I fear that this executive's words are accurate about many young adults now emerging into broader culture. While there is more information available for the taking than at any other time in history, there seems to be less understanding of truth than ever before. Few young adults of this generation seem to have been captured by the call to be true heroes in their own lives.

Scripture talks often about the perils of neglecting to guide a child. Many are easily led as sheep to moral or spiritual slaughter, so to speak, because they have never been taught to examine their values or think for themselves. Ignorance and mental weakness bring poverty of soul and set people on a dangerous course. When adults lack character, their children have little chance of developing it themselves. But the opposite is also true. The home, in fact, is the ideal training ground for heroes.

Scripture commands us to love God with our whole being—heart and soul and mind (Matthew 22:37). And raising children to be true heroes involves attention to developing all three aspects of a child.

God has created human beings with an immense capacity to use their brains to study, understand, create, invent, and debate. Consequently, one of the most vital forms of stewardship we have as parents is to take responsibility for developing our children's minds. Like a muscle that needs to be stretched and used over and over again to become strong, so their brains must be stretched and exercised, trained to not only acquire information but to also analyze and apply it.

There is more to developing heroes, of course, than simply developing minds. Children also need to have their hearts inspired and their imaginations engaged, to be exposed to the possibilities of heroism and the values that fuel it. They need to see heroism in action and grow up on stories of people who have lived valiant lives.

Books can't be beat as sources of such stories. Think about creating a library full of inspiring stories—biographies, great literature, historical classics—and helping your children develop an appetite for such books. You can even more effectively communicate the importance of such books to your children by reading them aloud. Not only will your children benefit from this practice but I guarantee you will be encouraged as well. Children who are read to invariably fall in love with reading and books. This practice increases vocabulary, promotes a broad understanding of the world, and helps children become well versed in history, religion, philosophy, politics, languages, and many other facets of education.

The next step is to take the information your children gain from reading and push them to engage with it. Require them to come to their own conclusions about the stories they are reading. The more they own such a process for themselves, the more ready they will be to enact it when they embark upon their adult lives. If thought and engagement are valued in the home and around the family table, then it will become a cherished value for life.

Although exposure to the stories of history and literature is important, there is no greater source of "hero training" than God's Word. Scripture teaches everything children most need in order to follow the hero's way:

- God's attributes, God's character, and God's Word so that they can have a true understanding and love for their Creator, Redeemer, and Sustainer
- Biblical morality so that they can build their lives on true foundations for relationships, professional decisions, and spiritual pursuits
- Wisdom, which synthesizes an understanding of both of the above items and realizes them in a thoughtful and intentional way
- The very best stories of courage and endurance to inspire them and engage their hearts

So let Scripture be written on the "tablet of your heart" (Proverbs 7:3) and on your children's hearts as well. Make it available everywhere they look in your home. Give them their own Bibles and read its stories together. Learn Scripture yourself so that it comes out of your mouth as naturally as breath.

And then, if you truly want to inspire your children to be heroes, do your best to be a hero yourself. Again, this doesn't mean you have to go out and fight bad guys. It doesn't mean you have to be perfect, either. But it does mean you need to recognize the power of your example.

Children learn heroism from watching their parents loving, giving, practicing unselfishness and self-sacrifice, acting with courage, refusing to complain about hardship, confessing sin, asking for forgiveness, and practicing integrity on a daily basis. When a mom or dad or another role model determines to live the noblest life possible—to be as much like Jesus as possible and seek to know Him better every day—children's appetites for righteousness grow and they get a taste for what true heroism looks like.

Don't underestimate the power of this kind of living. Throughout history, when parents attend to the education of their own minds and souls and those of their children, a country flourishes. That is how important the work of home is today, tomorrow, and forever. The ideals that are lived, taught, and cherished will determine the future of any culture, family, or individual. What an incredible stewardship opportunity—to shape a home where heroes are made.

At Home in the Word

1.   *"Whatever was written in earlier times was written for our instruction, so that through perseverance and the encouragement of the Scriptures we might have hope" (Romans 15:4).*

a. The Bible is living history, full of stories of faith. What heroes from Scripture speak most powerfully to you and your family members? List at least three.

b. Many of the heroes in the Bible are far from perfect. They make plenty of mistakes and get in trouble with God. What makes them heroes? What do their stories tell us about being heroes in our own lives?

2. *"Since we have so great a cloud of witnesses surrounding us, let us also lay aside every encumbrance and the sin which so easily entangles us, and let us run with endurance the race that is set before us, fixing our eyes on Jesus, the author and perfecter of faith"* (Hebrews 12:1-2).

a. More traditional churches honor the saints—great heroes of the faith who forged paths of spiritual goodness in their time. What "saints"—people of great faith either in past centuries or the current day—inspire you? List several people you especially admire.

b. Why do you think that being aware of the great "cloud of witnesses" around us enables us to "lay aside every encumbrance"? In what ways does thinking about faithful people who have gone before you help in your own spiritual journey? If possible, give a personal example.

3. *"In the beginning was the Word, and the Word was with God, and the Word was God" (John 1:1).*

a. God's voice has spoken in a special way through Jesus. As you think of the people in history who are important role models to you, have you thought of Jesus in that way? Write down some ways that Jesus influenced history. Would you consider Him a hero? Why or why not?

b. The voices whose words you hear the most will shape your thinking and inform your own vocabulary. What voices do you tend to listen to most—people you know, TV or radio, Internet sites, social media, books, newspapers? Write down the three that influence you most. (Be honest.) Are there any you should change?

4. *"Indeed, I brought you up from the land of Egypt and ransomed you from the house of slavery, and I sent before you Moses, Aaron and Miriam" (Micah 6:4).*

    a. Think through times in the past when God has been faithful to you. What happened? Write out the story in a short paragraph. If you can't think of a personal story, it's okay to write down a story you have heard.

    b. Often the Israelites got in trouble with God because they forgot His good deeds to them. Can you think of times in your life when you did this? Why do you think remembering is so important? What are some practical strategies we can develop to help our memory of God's goodness?

Bringing It Home

WHAT IS YOUR BIGGEST CHALLENGE FOR JULY?

The heat of summer always begins to take its toll on me come July. I have adverse reactions to hot, humid days, so I have learned to be attentive to finding a cool place. Sometimes the best way to live well is simply to plan ahead and attend to what you know you and your family need.

*What do you struggle with in July? What are you doing
(or could you do) to overcome that struggle?*

_____

_____

_____

_____

_____

July Anniversaries, Birthdays, and Holidays

In our family, we celebrate the Fourth of July enthusiastically—usually with my famous fried chicken for lunch and a cookout with friends for dinner. We love celebrating the grand story of our nation's early beginnings.

List your own family events for July:

_____

_____

_____

_____

To Read or Watch in July

Picture Books: Cynthia Rylant brings her childhood in Appalachia to life through her exuberant and colorful books. From the wistfulness of *When I Was Young in the Mountains,* illustrated by Diane Goode (1982), to the rip-roaring excitement of *The Relatives Came,* illustrations by Stephen Gammell (1985), these books capture the simplicity and joy of a past America.

Literature and Nonfiction: July is an excellent time to catch up on American history and culture. Mark Twain wrote many thoughtful, humorous stories about nineteenth-century rural America, including *The Adventures of Tom Sawyer* (1876), *Adventures of Huckleberry Finn* (1885), and *A Connecticut Yankee in King Arthur's Court* (1889). Esther Hoskins Forbes's *Johnny Tremain* (1943) and Jean Lee Latham's *Carry On, Mr. Bowditch* (1955) are examples of young adult fiction set in Revolutionary-era America, while Harold Keith's *Rifles for Watie* (1957) and Irene Hunt's *Across Five Aprils* (1964) are set during the American Civil War.

Movies and Series: *Gettysburg* (1993) is a superb four-hour epic that takes the viewer through a profound and moving depiction of the Battle of Gettysburg in 1863, a pivotal clash in the Civil War. Lighter and perhaps more suitable for younger viewers is the film adaptation of the previously mentioned *Johnny Tremain* (1957). The charming animated feature *An American Tail* (1986) tells the story of early twentieth-century immigration to the United States through the eyes of a family of Russian mice.

Consider which of these or other books, television series, or films you could enjoy with your family in July.

PEOPLE PRIORITIES FOR JULY

July is cookout month for the Clarksons, and we have many families over to our home. We love serving our local community of friends in that way. We've even been known to invite friends over who bring their sleeping bags to share a night out under the stars on our deck. Colorado decks are wonderful for making sweet memories. But backyards, front yards, apartment balconies, porches, and even parks can work that way, too, no matter where you live. What casual outdoor evening can you dream up to delight everyone?

What people do you plan to prioritize in July? Who do you miss seeing and would love to catch up with?

_____

_____

_____

_____

_____

August

THE STORY OF US
Shaping and Celebrating Family Culture

*Our heritage and ideals, our code and standards—
the things we live by and teach our children—are preserved or
diminished by how freely we exchange ideas and feelings.*

WALT DISNEY

The flicker of candlelight, the luscious aromas of hot cinnamon rolls and strong coffee, and lots of noise and laughter filled the kitchen as we tucked into breakfast together. Thus began our twenty-fifth year of celebrating the story and heritage of our family. Family Day, as we call it, is a time of remembering who we are as a family as well as documenting what God has done in our family and committing to Him our hopes for the future.

It all started back when our kids were little, with a passage from the Old Testament. We read that Joshua, commissioned with the difficult task of overseeing the Hebrew people after Moses' death, knew that his people needed to constantly be reminded of who they were—God's chosen people who had been called to possess the land God had provided for them. So Joshua came up with a unique way to make the abstract truth of God's promises very tangible and real to the Israelites. They would gather large memorial stones and place them as a monument to stand throughout many generations, documenting God's faithfulness to His people (see Joshua 4).

Clay and I wanted our children to have that kind of palpable reminder of God's commitment to our family. So we began setting aside an annual day to name and remember the important events of the previous twelve months. In the very beginning we used actual pebbles for our "memorial stones" and had the kids draw pictures of the events. As the kids grew older, we just listed the events, although we persisted in calling the items in the list "stones." We thanked God for every stone and preserved all of our pictures and lists in a family album. This tradition gave our children an expectation that we would always be purposeful and intentional about who our family was, what we stood for, and how we would approach our future.

We still have Family Day every year even though our children are now grown and living away from home, and we still begin the day by listing our "memorial stones" together. This practice reminds us not only of God's faithfulness to us individually and as a family but also of the fact that we are inextricably tied to one another, bound in loyalty. It is a renewed annual commitment to always be there for one another. Our Family Day celebration also helps us reaffirm our family culture—our values, traditions, tastes, words, and music, and the infinite amount of other things that define us as Clarksons.

Throughout the Old Testament, God was always commanding the Israelites to *remember*. His feast days were all about recalling what He had provided in His faithfulness to His chosen people, and they were admonished to remember His teachings as well. I believe He wants us to remember, too, because forgetfulness is the fastest way to failure. Remembering is an act of rooting ourselves deep in the soil of our spiritual heritage.

When our children were growing up, we wanted to empower them by repeating the stories of God's miraculous intervention throughout history and in our own lives. We shared with them how God had taken our loaves and fish—a desire to start a ministry with no money, no books, and no conferences—and multiplied them beyond our wildest imaginations. We created a constant narrative of God's desire to use them to change the world. And throughout the years we used our annual Family Day lists to affirm the little miracles along the way.

Now that my children are grown, they have owned that narrative for themselves. They remember His faithfulness in their lives when they are tempted to lose hope. They take joy in the many small graces of normal, uneventful living. And it is clear to me that God has enlarged the hearts of each of my children to trust Him for things far beyond their understanding or ability to achieve on their own.

Thanking God in the circle of family on Family Day has become one of my sweetest moments each year. My heart swells as I hear the deep voices of my boys praying fervently for all of us and the excited voices of my girls speaking in anticipation of how He will be faithful the next year. I love knowing that these beloved ones in whose lives I have invested for so long are now living vibrant lives of faith. And almost as precious to me is the awareness that all of them love and support one another. They affirm one another in their dreams of bringing God's light to their own arenas because they know our family history and story so well and because our shared love is at the core of our lives.

Through trials and challenges, ups and downs, our now-adult children say that those many days of remembering together have given them strength to forge lives of faith. Looking back, we can perceive some of the patterns in the tapestry of our lives and see the ways we picked up the threads from others who went before us. Now my children are using the same threads for their own lives, adding new colors and textures to the mix, weaving the story in rhythms of faith established long before them. They are aware of being caught up into the beautiful garment of faith being sewn throughout the ages.

Don't you want that for your family too? This month, consider how you might celebrate your own family culture and story of faith.

What is your heritage, your legacy? What makes you you? More important, what has God been doing through you? Don't forget to remember!

At Home in the Word

1. *"The lovingkindness of the* LORD *is from everlasting to everlasting on those who fear Him, and His righteousness to children's children, to those who keep His covenant and remember His precepts to do them" (Psalm 103:17-18).*

   a. The story you are telling with your family today started long before you and will continue long after you. Consider what it means for your family to live not just for the immediate moment but also as an example for those who come after you. Name three aspects of your family life today that you hope will become part of your heritage.

   b. Verse 17 above says that God is full of lovingkindness over many generations for those who obey Him. But what if you or your family *haven't* always obeyed Him or kept His covenant? If you are concerned about negative elements in your family's past, list them here and pray over them. What would it take for you to tap into the fountain of God's grace and change your family heritage?

2. *"Hear, my son, your father's instruction and do not forsake your mother's teaching; indeed, they are a graceful wreath to your head and ornaments about your neck" (Proverbs 1:8-9).*

    a. There is a sense in this verse that what we've learned from good instruction will be a visible attribute (a wreath or an ornament) for the rest of our lives. Can you think of qualities passed on to you that make up your "graceful wreath" of wisdom?

    b. What methods do you generally use to train up your children in goodness? Do you present your instruction as a gift, or is it more often received as a punishment? Do you think your instruction is effective, or would you like to try an alternative? Why or why not?

3. *"Honor your father and your mother, that your days may be prolonged in the land which the LORD your God gives you" (Exodus 20:12).*

    a. This Scripture explicitly ties success in life with honoring one's parents. No matter where we are in life, we all have parents—whether actual fathers and mothers or other authority figures—to whom we owe respect. Who are these people in your life? Name three specific ways you can show them honor. If there are elements of your family history that make it difficult for you to honor certain authority figures, name at least one way you can show honor to them without being dishonest or dishonoring your own experience.

b. We live in a time of incivility and lack of respect. How can you teach your children honor for you and for others? List two or three possibilities.

4. *"Indeed, my heritage is beautiful to me" (Psalm 16:6).*

a. God desires to create a beautiful heritage with you and your family, both for future generations after you and for the family of His bride, the church. Write down at least three ways that God has blessed you and your family and take a moment to thank Him for those things.

b. How do you typically talk about your home, your family, your husband, and your children in front of others? It's natural to vent a little sometimes, but a habit of complaining can perpetuate negative feelings. Write down at least one positive thing you can honestly say about each family member in the next week and make a point of saying it.

Bringing It Home

WHAT IS YOUR BIGGEST CHALLENGE FOR AUGUST?

When our kids were young, our household always got a little crazy this time of year. Our kids were determined to cram in every last vacation experience before school was upon us, while I was trying to prepare for the new school year. Instead of letting myself be overwhelmed in those last few weeks, I eventually learned to enjoy every minute, knowing that someday I would look back and miss those times. (I do!)

What do you struggle with in August? What are you doing (or could you do) to overcome that struggle?

_____

_____

_____

_____

_____

AUGUST ANNIVERSARIES, BIRTHDAYS, AND HOLIDAYS

August is usually the month for our Family Day, which always includes a picnic and a hike as well as our annual time of remembrance. It's also my birthday month, and my sweet family always treats me to a fun day. A Sunday afternoon teatime is my favorite way to celebrate—with cards, prayers, and spoken blessings. I always feel especially blessed in August.

List your own family events for August:

_____

_____

_____

_____

_____

To Read or Watch in August

Picture Books: Barbara Cooney, a Caldecott award–winning writer and artist, wrote and illustrated numerous wonderful picture books, many evoking the pleasant tranquility of summer. Favorites include *Miss Rumphius* (1982), *Roxaboxen* (with text by Alice McLerran, 1991), and *Island Boy* (1988).

Literature and Nonfiction: My children have many wonderful memories of reading classic tales of adventure and bravery. Sarah read Robert Louis Stevenson's *Kidnapped* (1886) aloud to her little brothers, who loved the swashbuckling derring-do. Other enjoyable classics include Stevenson's *Treasure Island* (1883) and Johann Wyss's *The Swiss Family Robinson* (1812).

Movies and Series: *Babe* (1995) is the irresistible tale of a pig born for greatness. Barely escaping the slaughterhouse, young Babe is won as a prize by the modest Farmer Hoggett, who quickly falls for the intelligent and winsome swine. Replete with singing mice and noble border collies (who teach Babe how to herd sheep), this film is sure to win your heart.

Consider which of these or other books, television series, or films you could enjoy with your family in August.

People Priorities for August

Because Family Day is one of the rare times these days when everyone is home at the same time, my August priority is us—strengthening our bonds of friendship and fellowship. I am so blessed to be part of this silly, crazy, wonderful group of people I call my family. I try to enjoy each moment, not becoming overwhelmed by the messes and dirty dishes, but celebrating each memory we have made together.

What people do you plan to prioritize in August? What important relationships do you want to remember and celebrate?

_____

_____

_____

_____

_____

September

WHEN SEASONS CHANGE
Gathering In for Home and Soul

Be prepared, and prepare yourself, you and all your companies
that are assembled about you, and be a guard for them.

EZEKIEL 38:7

Furrowed eyebrows above large dark eyes was the signal to me as a mom that something was not right with one of my children. Like my other precious ones, she had faced the challenge of growing up more or less in public and was feeling exposed and fragile, inadequate to live into such a pressured role.

God has blessed our family with the opportunity to interact with so many people from so many different walks of life and to touch others with our ministry, but I had learned very quickly that this was not always easy for my children. And this particular child had begun to grow into a challenging point of adolescence and especially needed attention and affirmation from me.

"Mama, do you ever feel like a hypocrite when your life is so . . . visible? Doesn't it get hard to keep on writing and speaking about your ideals when your failures are right out there for people to see? Do you ever feel disqualified?"

She went on: "I really need to get away from the voices and eyes of the world right now. Can't we hole up in the house for a few days and just be ourselves, with all our warts and weirdnesses?" We ended up doing just that.

Truth be told, I could totally relate to what my sweet daughter was saying. I feel like quitting ministry about ten times a week! I am just a normal Christian woman wanting to love Jesus and live according to His example, and God simply called me into a more public place than I would ever have chosen.

How well I know what my child was discovering—the vulnerability that comes from being a leader, from publicly standing firm on an ideal. You put your neck out and stand for principles, and yet you are still only human and make mistakes along the way. Not everyone understands, and there is plenty of criticism to face in the journey. Add to that our breakneck, high-pressure, high-consumption contemporary culture and it's easy to reach a place where we feel depleted, needing a place of safety and refuge, desperately thirsty for emotional, physical, and spiritual water to refresh us.

The way I have been able to bear all this (most of the time) is to make our fallibility a part of our message. I've always been up-front about the reality that I and my family aren't perfect or always strong. We fall down and mess up like any other family. But even when we've blown it, struggled with the dark side of life, or wallowed in our own sin and selfishness, God has been faithful to us. The heart of my message is that God still redeems every moment, every mistake, and every failure.

It is a risk to stand for something, to seek after the holy ways of God, to keep going when you are weary to the bone, to love when you feel hurt and rejected, especially by those who call themselves Christians. Every one of us will be called in some capacity to live into a call and will face this struggle in some way.

That's why all of us need a place of escape from time to time. We need a home—but not just any home. Home needs to be a haven of safety, acceptance, and unconditional love, a place where we can rest and find refuge from all the devastating and depleting parts of life. When the storms and difficulties come, home should be the first line of defense against despair. This is why we must guard our homes as if they were our very lifelines. Because they are!

It is impossible to have any influence in the world, to speak with a voice of love, grace, and truth, if we don't have a foundation of stability and peace from which we can go out into the world. Home creates the starting point for any sense of belonging we will have. The kind of message that truly transforms people comes from those who have rooted themselves in a sacred sanctuary where burdens, failures, disappointments, and insecurities are not judged, but held in holy trust. My children know they will be okay when they are required to be strong, to face struggles, and to admit their limitations because they know where they come from and where they can always return if the need arises. This reality of home as a safe, welcoming, restorative refuge is foundational to everything we accomplish as individuals and as a family.

Our homes are also such a place for strangers who come in from outside. Many people we encounter in our lives have no idea of what it means to have a home, of how a home-centered identity transforms the soul. Our homes are potential incubation chambers for growing Christ-infused individuals. In our homes, we have the opportunity to bring about incredible grace and goodness, both for those who live there and those who visit.

To have that kind of home, intentional preparation is required. For a home to be well readied to receive anyone in any season, we must plan, store up, allocate, and put systems in place that protect what is precious to us. We must gather in season so that we can reap out of season—a perfect message for a month when leaves begin to turn and the first hints of winter begin to arrive.

This doesn't mean that all the work of preparation must be done at once—or done in a particular month. Rather it is a constant adding of this and that, of one piece here and another there. Every season allows for such moments. And there is great grace in the midst.

Today I challenge you: How will you make your home a place of refuge? How will you provide a place of unconditional love where secrets can be shared and carried as a holy trust? How will you provide quiet and rest, recreation and inspiration for those within your walls? How will you keep the messages of a frenzied culture at bay so that the truth heard in your home will be that which instructs, comforts, gives insight, and shows love to those who hunger for peace and restoration?

How will you plan your home? Go forth and prepare.

At Home in the Word

1. *"Go to the ant, O sluggard, observe her ways and be wise, which, having no chief, officer or ruler, prepares her food in the summer and gathers her provision in the harvest" (Proverbs 6:6-8).*

    a. The ant is seen as wise because even without any assistance or advice, it prepares and takes care of itself so that it can survive and thrive. What are you doing right now to take care of yourself physically, emotionally, and spiritually? What support systems and resources do you have in place?

b. Do you think there is such a thing as overpreparing or being too self-sufficient? How can you balance your responsibility for taking care of yourself with your need to trust God and others? Do you tend to lean too far in either direction?

2. *"Do not store up for yourselves treasures on earth, where moth and rust destroy, and where thieves break in and steal. But store up for yourselves treasures in heaven, where neither moth nor rust destroys, and where thieves do not break in or steal; for where your treasure is, there your heart will be also"* *(Matthew 6:19-21).*

a. As you put effort into preparation, what are you anticipating? Are you putting your hope in passing things, or are you and your family investing in the Kingdom, toward an inheritance that will last for eternity? How does this view affect your approach to relationships, faith, personal memories, discipleship, family activities, and every aspect of your life? Write down three things you can do right now to strengthen the invisible strings that tie your hearts together.

b. In your home, what is your family's ethic for possessions? How do you decide what is enough, and how do you teach your children about money and material things?

3. *"For this reason you also must be ready; for the Son of Man is coming at an hour when you do not think He will"* *(Matthew 24:44).*

a. What do you think it means to be ready for Jesus? What would a home that is ready look like? What would happen there?

b. With the hustle and bustle of a busy family life, it's so easy to get distracted from the most important things. What are some practical ways you can foster a sense of spiritual readiness in your home and set an example for your children?

4. *"She rises also while it is still night and gives food to her household. . . . She is not afraid of the snow for her household, for all her household are clothed with scarlet. . . . Strength and dignity are her clothing, and she smiles at the future"* *(Proverbs 31:15, 21, 25).*

a. It's impossible to always be prepared for every eventuality, but most of us can prepare better than we do. What are some ways you have let life take you by surprise in the past rather than preemptively preparing for a changing home environment? What steps could you have taken to prepare better? (Be sure to give yourself plenty of grace as you consider this. Don't beat yourself up!)

b. Looking ahead at the next season of your life (toddlers? school choice? teenagers? retirement?), write down three or four challenges you can reasonably expect. Then jot down some ways you can be proactive rather than reactive in meeting each challenge.

Bringing It Home

What Is Your Biggest Challenge for September?

When our children were younger, getting everyone—myself included—into back-to-school mode after a summer of fun was always a challenge for me. I found that making a fairly strict schedule and sticking to it helped immensely, especially for the first few weeks. Even if I didn't follow my plan for the whole year, it got everyone back in sync.

*What do you struggle with in September? What are you
doing (or could you do) to overcome that struggle?*

_____

_____

_____

_____

_____

SEPTEMBER ANNIVERSARIES, BIRTHDAYS, AND HOLIDAYS

September holds little in the way of significant events for our family. However, we always make a point of taking drives, having picnics, seeing sights, and enjoying the last lingering days of summer before fall arrives.

List your own family events for September:

_____

_____

_____

_____

_____

To Read or Watch in September

Picture Books: Jeff Brumbeau's *The Quiltmaker's Gift* (2000) and *The Quiltmaker's Journey* (2004) capture the beauty of a life pieced together bit by bit. Gail de Marcken's gorgeous illustrations of quilts and quilting provide a treat for the eyes and the imagination.

Literature and Nonfiction: Anna Sewell's *Black Beauty* (1877) is a unique story told from the perspective of a handsome black horse in Victorian England. In following Beauty's journey from an idyllic life on a farm through a succession of jobs and masters, it also teaches lessons of kindness and empathy. In a similar vein, Walter Farley's *The Black Stallion* (1941) follows young Alec Ramsay, a British boy who is stranded on a desert island with a beautiful Arabian horse. The story (and nineteen more books in The Black Stallion series) follows their consequent friendship, their rescue, and their escapades following their return to civilization. Nathan in particular loved *The Black Stallion* and really responded when I told him he needed to take the reins of my discipline in order to win his race.

Movies and Series: We Clarksons love uplifting, family-affirming TV series. Two in particular are wonderful additions to any household. *Road to Avonlea* (1990–1996), a spin-off of the previously mentioned *Anne of Green Gables* films, is a heartwarming collection of stories about the King family, set on Canada's tranquil Prince Edward Island at the turn of the twentieth century.

Similar in nature but set in Victorian England, *Lark Rise to Candleford* (2008–2011), based on Flora Thompson's 1945 auto-biographical novel, follows the early adult life of Laura Timmins, an assistant postmistress for the local post office, and her keen observations of rural Oxfordshire. In recent years, watching *Lark Rise* has become an annual September event for the girls in our family.

For horse lovers in your family, both *Black Beauty* and *The Black*

Stallion were translated into wonderful films. We liked *Black Beauty* (1994), but we *loved* the 1979 movie version of *The Black Stallion,* with beautiful, poetic scenes of boy and horse alone together and Mickey Rooney making an impact as the trainer who taught Alec how to race.

Consider which of these or other books, television series, or films you could enjoy with your family in September.

PEOPLE PRIORITIES FOR SEPTEMBER

Because of the need to help my kids get back into the swing of the school year, they were the focus of most of my attention in September when they were home. I also liked to focus on launching us all happily into the coming autumn season: decorating the house with fall plants, cooking fall food (pumpkin muffins! homemade applesauce! simmering soups and fragrant bread!) and stocking up on staples to carry us through the winter.

What people do you plan to prioritize in September?
How can you create pleasure on these beautiful fall days and
help those you love move gracefully into a new season?
(Why not try a new fall recipe and invite someone
over to enjoy the delectable results?)

_____

_____

_____

_____

October

HOME IS BEST
Serving Life within Your Walls

To invite someone into your home
Is to take charge of their happiness
For as long as they are under your roof.

JEAN ANTHELME BRILLAT-SAVARIN

In many parts of the nation—and certainly in our little corner of Colorado—October is the month when the temperatures drop and a chill is felt in the air. And yet October is invariably a warm month for me, filled with delightful good times. For this chapter, I'd like to invite you into my home for a little visit.

Let's step over the threshold and through my double front doors. I recently had them painted red—a deep crimson suffused with hints of vermilion to catch the light flickering off the few remaining shimmery leaves of the aspen grove outside. Red is the color of the heart, and I want our home to be a place where the heart is captured by the beauty of belonging. Red is also the color of warmth and vibrancy, capturing the celebration and feasting that happen regularly within the walls of our home.

As you pass through the parlor, I invite you to enter my living room. Take a seat in one of my enormous paisley hostess chairs, and as you sink in and get comfortable, I'll go put the teakettle on. While I'm away, I hope the flickering candles spread throughout the room will light a fire of joy in your heart as you catch strains of the tranquil classical music gracefully filling the expanse of the vaulted ceiling above. Perhaps as you look around, the candlelight will reflect off of one of the many bird figurines decorating my living room.

Many years ago, when I was struggling as a young mother and missionary in Austria, far away from home, I cried out to the Lord in a moment of need. And at that moment a beautiful sparrow hopped up on my windowsill, chirped a lovely song, and then flittered away to some other appointment. Ever since then, I have been visited by beautiful birds when I am tempted to despair. So I keep reproductions of my feathered friends around to remind me that the light of Christ is incarnated into the world all around me, and all I must do to see it is be attentive.

Now that we have our cups of tea in hand, please accompany me to our family great room. It's only just past the staircase and the piano. I love that piano. My father, a jazz aficionado and dedicated amateur trumpet player, traded his beloved trumpet for our upright piano. Whenever I pass it, I can faintly hear the echoes of his singing and playing, a ghost of a memory revisiting itself gently upon me. I also think of my kids when I see that piano; they all took lessons on it, and when they're home they love to gather around it to sing and play. It delights my mama heart to see them enjoying filling the rafters with harmony and melody. Music seeps up through the soil of our family, past and present. Without fail, if you wait long enough in our home, music will begin to stream in from somewhere or other.

I hope you'll make yourself comfortable on our old-fashioned leather sofa here in the great room. It's got cushions you could disappear into, doesn't it? As I light a fire in the fireplace, perhaps you'll notice the sea of deep twilight blue on all the surrounding walls enveloping you. To me it's like an engulfing ocean. I like to think that when we read out loud together, as we often do in this room, we are embarking onto a sea of imagination and curiosity. Everyone needs a good space to become lost in a story.

The aroma of fresh-baked chocolate chip cookies is wafting from the kitchen. Excuse me while I check on them; I'll only be a minute. Or better yet, why don't you come with me? Everybody else does. Whenever I cook dinner or bake a treat, I know that all I have to do is wait. Before I know it, the scent of hot-out-of-the-oven bread or eggs and bacon on the griddle will draw my offspring from the four corners of our home. Isn't that amazing?

Food is like a magnet. I have always known that feasting is one of my most important tools for winning my children's hearts. October is such a wonderful time for it, too, with all those great fall flavors— hot chocolate, cinnamon apple cider, pumpkin pie, and an assortment of other treats. I'm glad you came today so that I can treat you.

Now that I've liberated the cookies from the oven, let's take the plate back into the great room to enjoy with our tea. I see that you've picked up my coffee-table picture book—I love that one! Our home has always been a gallery for our favorite art. Behind you on the wall is an original print by a beloved Austrian artist, Luigi Kasimir. The gentle mountain scene is typical of his work. Clay and I fell in love with Kasimir's art when we lived in Vienna and collected many of his works. They have traveled with us to many different homes, always reminding us of our time overseas.

One of the things I love best about art is that it can open up a window to a different world, creating a new space for us to inhabit. When I am lost in the troubles of my own life, the beautiful artwork throughout my home allows me to imaginatively place myself in a place beyond the everyday. It affirms experientially what I know to be true logically—that God works beyond our capacity and draws us through His Spirit into a life of incredible color, beauty, and breadth.

Watch out! Kelsey, our golden retriever, has sniffed out the cookies and is looking for her opportunity to sweep in and snatch a couple away. That dog may be an "olden golden," but she hasn't lost any of her capacity for mischief. When it comes down to it, she's not really that useful, but she's ours and we love her.

Isn't that the way it is with our Lord? We often overestimate our value in the world and obsess about the consequences of our actions. But sometimes I wonder if God sees us more as mischievous golden retrievers trying to steal cookies and gives us grace according to the fact that although we have earned nothing, He loves us and we are His. I don't know how theologically accurate that thought is, but I do find it comforting.

Oh dear, is it already time for you to go? I feel so honored you joined me here. My home is my habitation of grace, and the more I share it, the more I am empowered to spread that grace to others. I hope that when you leave, you'll find your life has been enriched— not because I have done anything special, but because Christ has filled this environment with His incarnational presence, and by our communing together, we have met Him here.

Be blessed as you go out, and may you be inspired to create such warmth in the rooms of your own home.

At Home in the Word

1. *"Jesus sent Peter and John, saying, 'Go and prepare the Passover for us, so that we may eat it.' . . . When the hour had come, He reclined at the table, and the apostles with Him. And He said to them, 'I have earnestly desired to eat this Passover with you before I suffer'" (Luke 22:8, 14-15).*

   a. Why do you think Jesus felt it was so important to share a meal together with His friends before He died? What does this tell you about the importance of mealtimes in a home?

b. Jesus took pains to plan a Passover celebration for His disciples—in other words, He showed them hospitality. What are some simple, specific things you can do to make mealtimes feel special for your family and your friends? Brainstorm a few ways you could do this with a minimum investment of time and money—so that you're more likely to actually do it.

2. *"Do not neglect to show hospitality to strangers, for by this some have entertained angels without knowing it" (Hebrews 13:2).*

a. The best way to provide meaningful hospitality to anyone— friend or stranger—is to create regular habits of welcome. This could be anything from developing a signature dish to decorating your home to putting together a basket of supplies for overnight guests. Name three things you think you can easily incorporate into your life right now.

b. What "buts" rise in your mind when you think of sharing your home with others? What worries you? What are you afraid of? Write these out and consider how you might overcome these hesitations with God's help.

3. *"He poured water into the basin, and began to wash the disciples' feet and to wipe them with the towel with which He was girded. . . . So when He had washed their feet, and taken His garments and reclined at the table again, He said to them, 'Do you know what I have done to you? You call Me Teacher and Lord; and you are right, for so I am. If I then, the Lord and the Teacher, washed your feet, you also ought to wash one another's feet'" (John 13:5, 12-14).*

   a. This passage gives us a vivid picture of the connection between acts of service (even the most menial or unpleasant) and relationships. List at least three ways you choose to serve the ones you love in your home—and at least one way you could serve them better.

   b. People have different responses to being served by others. Some act entitled, expecting the service as their due. Others (like Peter) become embarrassed or even refuse to be served. Name two or three ways that responding graciously and gratefully to being served can strengthen relationships.

4. *"These things I have spoken to you, so that in Me you may have peace. In the world you have tribulation, but take courage; I have overcome the world"* (John 16:33).

    a. Describe the most peaceful, restful home or place you have ever visited. What made it peaceful? How could you recreate those elements in your own home?

    b. God is, of course, the ultimate Source of peace and encouragement. Consider some ways you can order your home and your life more intentionally to reflect His presence and His peace. This could include anything from home decor and atmosphere to the way you respond to conflict to the resources you provide. Write down two or three ideas.

Bringing It Home

WHAT IS YOUR BIGGEST CHALLENGE FOR OCTOBER?

I am, by all accounts, a lover of experience, and I've passed that love on to my kids. Because of the school year, October tends to be a quiet month, and I easily develop cabin fever. So I seek out new restaurants, parks, bookstores, and more to satisfy our hunger for new experiences.

*What do you struggle with in October? What are you
doing (or could you do) to overcome that struggle?*

_____

_____

_____

_____

_____

October Anniversaries, Birthdays, and Holidays

October tends to be a quieter time for the Clarkson family. However, we enjoy celebrating a big harvest festival toward the end of the month with friends. Evenings often find us enjoying community and fellowship at hero costume parties, Frito-pie evenings, or a potluck and game night with friends. Such a great time to light the home fires, cuddle up, and make memories. And don't forget the warm apple cider with cinnamon sticks!

List your own family events for October:

_____

_____

_____

_____

_____

To Read or Watch in October

Picture Books: Thomas Locker, a brilliant artist and storyteller, devoted his life to painting exquisite works, many of which have been used for children's books. *The Boy Who Held Back the Sea* (story by Lenny Hort, 1987) and *Rip Van Winkle* (Washington Irving's story adapted by Ashley Foehner, 2008) are family favorites.

Literature and Nonfiction: The United Kingdom has a penchant for producing wonderful authors of Christian fantasy. In the nineteenth century, George MacDonald, a preacher in the Scottish Highlands, wrote numerous works of fantasy, all filled with his ruminations on faith and imagination. *Phantastes* (1858), *At the Back of the North Wind* (1871), and *The Princess and the Goblin* (1872) are prime examples of his creative genius. Later on C. S. Lewis, an author deeply influenced by MacDonald, became the preeminent Christian writer of the twentieth century, writing multiple works of stunning clarity and poignancy. A few to start with include the seven novels in the fictional Chronicles of Narnia series (1950–1956), nonfiction books like *The Great Divorce* (1946), and the satirical masterpiece *The Screwtape Letters* (1942). J. R. R. Tolkien, a close friend of Lewis and fellow member of the creative writing group the Inklings, spent most of his career masterfully crafting his fantasy novels about Middle Earth, a fictional world realized in stunning detail by Tolkien, who even created original languages. *The Hobbit* (1937) and the three-part *Lord of the Rings* (1954–1955) are must-reads in our household.

Movies and Series: Because of my children's love for Christian fantasy, they were thrilled to see the film versions of some of their favorite works. Peter Jackson's version of *The Lord of the Rings*, while for more mature kids, is a standout. This epic eleven-hour version of Tolkien's timeless tale was released in three parts: *The Fellowship of the Ring* (2001), *The Two Towers* (2002), and *The Return of the King* (2003). The Chronicles of Narnia have been produced multiple times, including recent versions by Walt Disney and Walden Media, but our family favors the BBC version made in the 1980s, which we think captures the spirit of the books more effectively.

Consider which of these or other books, television series, or films you could enjoy with your family in October.

PEOPLE PRIORITIES FOR OCTOBER

My friends who live near me are usually my focus during October. I try my best to cultivate those local relationships, the friendships that will carry me in the long run. Afternoon teatimes and group gatherings for chili or soup are my favorite ways of doing this. When my children were living at home, I also made a priority of devising opportunities to show hospitality to their friends and potential friends.

What people do you plan to prioritize in October? What one event can you plan to make a memory with friends?

_____

_____

_____

_____

_____

November

BLESSED AND BLESSING
Grace, Gratitude, and Generosity

O give thanks to the LORD, for He is good;
For His lovingkindness is everlasting.

1 CHRONICLES 16:34

Sweeping, captivating tales of real men and women of courage who lived for God's glory in this world have always inspired my heart. I want to believe in modern-day miracles. I want to hold fast to stories of those who took risks to worship God, people who lived courageously and held fast against great odds, trusting in His goodness and His promises even in times of great trial. Our culture promotes self-centeredness, an obsession with the most trivial of daily distractions, and a dislike for anything transcendent. Society has lost its way and become diminished in the face of consumerism, materialism, and hedonism. The scary thing is I am just as easily ensnared by those things as anyone else. I seek out great stories because I need the reminder that it is within my grasp to be holy, to love mercy, and to walk humbly with my God (see Micah 6:8).

The early American settlement at Plymouth was the setting for such a tale. A small, dwindling group of seemingly frail individuals, invisible to the world at large, struggled to survive through disease, storms, and starvation. And yet even after only a small remnant of the original community remained, they still chose to worship and thank their creator God for His lovingkindness and mercy and provision.

These seemingly insignificant people were not invisible to God. Their tale has lived on to inspire generations to live a life of faith. They yearned to live intentional lives, engaging their hearts in practicing gratitude; they were devoted to joy, to celebrating the reality of God. The legacy of the Pilgrims is their testimony to the power of thankfulness and gratitude to transform any life. God took a small community's faithful acts of worship and turned their struggle and perseverance into an eternal work.

In our own time, the dominant culture teaches us that we should get what we want. Modern technology provides for any and every need we could have, and if we aren't able to receive something quickly, we are indignant. Instead of gratitude, there is dissatisfaction; instead of thankfulness, there is entitlement. And despite all the advantages that modern society provides, we still live in a time of great turmoil. Erosion of morality, economic pressures, the breakup of marriages, tragedies and disasters—no matter how advanced our world becomes, we will still always fall short of our desires.

The brokenness of the world will always be here, but so will God's grace. Gratitude is empowering; it recognizes that the world may be difficult, but there is something greater than the world, and to that truth it will cling with all its might. Ultimately, we are blessed beyond measure to know the risen Christ, to have confidence that our future is secure with Him for all eternity.

Someday, when we are with Him face-to-face, we will celebrate the greatest feast of all time. But now is our opportunity to celebrate our own now-but-not-yet feast of gratitude, to shout forth the light of God's presence into a dying world. Our thanksgiving recognizes the eternity present in the here and now; it is an act of radical faith that has the power to restart dying spiritual hearts. Just like those at

Plymouth, we are called to be faithful and to give thanks and trust that God can still use the acts of faithful people to turn the world upside down.

November is a great time of year to practice thanking God, not only for the things we have been given but also for the person He is, the ways He works in history, the stories He has left us as a pattern of faith, and the future hope we cherish because of His reality in our lives.

Consider the Pilgrims' reason for the conviction of their actions— the idea that men and women had the right to worship God according to their consciences, to do whatever was necessary to provide the legacy of faith in their families. The Pilgrims defiantly and unashamedly faced the hardship of the New World so that their children— and their children's children—would know what it means to speak the light of thanksgiving into the void of uncertainty and despair.

You, too, have the ability to do this; the power of the Holy Spirit is made strong in the most difficult points of your life. Is there an empty place in your life, a point of pain and lack? Speak gratitude and thanksgiving for God's presence and fill the void with words of praise. This Thanksgiving let your words be words of life.

I encourage you to dream with your family about how you might leave a legacy of faith, bringing His Kingdom to bear in this generation. I urge you to stand on the firm foundation of gratitude and thanksgiving and see God's grace seep into even the darkest crevices of your life. I am convinced you will be amazed by the harvest that even a mustard seed of praise will produce in your life and the lives of all those in your family.

At Home in the Word

1. *"The LORD bless you, and keep you; the LORD make His face shine on you, and be gracious to you; the LORD lift up His countenance on you, and give you peace" (Numbers 6:24-26).*

a. What connection do you see between blessing others and believing that God desires to bless you? What are some ways you can engage your heart more fully to trust in God's promises and His blessings?

b. Everyone needs to hear formal words of blessing and affirmation from time to time—words like "I am so blessed to have you as my child" or "May God smile on all of your days—you are so very dear to me." I consider this a way of speaking into the future lives of my children, my husband, and my friends. Write down several words and phrases of affirmation you could use later in an appropriate setting to bless another person. If necessary, practice them until they become second nature.

2. *"Rejoice always; pray without ceasing; in everything give thanks; for this is God's will for you in Christ Jesus" (1 Thessalonians 5:16-18).*

a. Cultivating a thankful heart is a sign of trust in God. What are some ways that you currently practice the habit of thanksgiving in your own life? What are some other ways of heightening your sense of gratitude?

b. How can you teach your children the habit of gratitude? List four or five strategies for teaching them not only to *say* thank you but also to mean it.

3. *"Devote yourselves to prayer, keeping alert in it with an attitude of thanksgiving" (Colossians 4:2).*

a. When and how do you pray together as a family? One-on-one with your spouse or a child? By yourself? Are you satisfied with the state of your prayer life? Why or why not?

b. Scripture is constantly telling us to stay alert and be ready. But how do you hold on to that sense of alert readiness over the long haul, especially when you are weary and overwhelmed? Brainstorm some strategies for keeping your spiritual eyes open. How do you think God responds to us when we don't?

4. *"You must each decide in your heart how much to give. And don't give reluctantly or in response to pressure, 'For God loves a person who gives cheerfully.' And God will generously provide all you need. Then you will always have everything you need and plenty left over to share with others. . . . He will provide and increase your resources and then produce a great harvest of generosity in you"* (2 Corinthians 9:7-8, 10, NLT).

   a. Can you remember a time in your life when you discovered how satisfying it can be to give to others? What were the circumstances? What has been the impact of that experience in your life?

   b. Brainstorm some ways to teach children to be generous and to acquaint them with the joys of giving. How can you practice generosity with your family?

Bringing It Home

WHAT IS YOUR BIGGEST CHALLENGE FOR NOVEMBER?

I am one of those people who are negatively affected by the shortening of the days and the coming cold. The best antidote I've found to the briefer daylight and the chill in the air is a dancing fire in the fireplace and a cup of cinnamon apple cider or hot chocolate shared with loved ones.

What do you struggle with in November? What are you doing (or could you do) to overcome that struggle?

_____

_____

_____

_____

November Anniversaries, Birthdays, and Holidays

Our family celebrates Thanksgiving with exuberance. Early morning happenings include a large breakfast of cinnamon rolls and eggs and some time in front of the TV watching the Macy's Thanksgiving Day Parade. From lunchtime onward we have guests trickle in for an enormous, hours-long meal with an abundance of courses—including turkey, two kinds of dressing, various potato dishes, Le Sueur brand green peas (we accept no substitutes!), cranberry sauce, squash casserole, and pumpkin pie. This has become one of the best ways to meet new people in our community.

List your own family events for November:

_____

_____

_____

_____

To Read or Watch in November

Picture Books: Donald Hall's *Ox-Cart Man* (1979) is a wonderful story about an itinerant merchant in New England who goes from town to town selling his goods and observing the passing seasons. Barbara Cooney's folk-art-style illustrations add to the charm.

Literature and Nonfiction: Louisa May Alcott is beloved in our home. She wrote from her own experience of family life in nineteenth-century New England during the American Civil War. *Little Women* (1868) is her best-known work, but we also love *Little Men* (1871) and *Jo's Boys* (1886).

Movies and Series: Early in our marriage, Clay and I fell in love with *Babette's Feast* (1987), a Danish film about a stranger staying with two women in a small village who throws a magnificent feast for her two benefactors and their friends. Though the film moves at a very gradual pace, the mystery slowly builds into a moving climax, a startling revelation of the power of art and the beauty that can come from gratitude and blessing others.

Consider which of these or other books, television series, or films you could enjoy with your family in November.

People Priorities for November

My firstborn son, Joel, celebrates his birthday in November. It is such a delight for us to take time to bless him and celebrate his life. Even better, Joel's birthday often corresponds with a trip our family takes to Breckenridge, a ski town deep in the Rocky Mountains—so both the birthday and the trip have become highly anticipated annual family events.

What people do you plan to prioritize in November? Who comes to mind first when you think of those you are thankful for?

_____

_____

_____

_____

_____

December

THE RHYTHM OF CELEBRATION
Seasons of Rejoicing in Family Life

I will honour Christmas in my heart, and try to keep it all the year.
CHARLES DICKENS

As I gaze back over the decades of my life, I can see so many experiences that have shaped my view of the world. But none has had quite the effect on me as living with Clay as a young couple in Vienna, Austria. Our lives there brought us a variety of faith-stretching lessons as we were confronted by the challenges of living and working in a foreign culture. My idealistic, conviction-laden husband found himself a junior pastor at the International Chapel of Vienna, and we quickly began to build connections with the expatriate community there.

Because Vienna had one of the highest costs of living in the world at the time, we struggled to find a suitable place to live with a two-and-a-half-year-old princess, a bouncing baby boy on the way, and a desperately needed au pair. After a challenging search, Clay and I finally found a small house tucked away in a northern suburb of the city. Our crooked little gray-stucco bungalow boasted nine hundred square feet divided between five people, and we stumbled over one another in the small space as we attempted to craft a lovely life. That house was a daily adventure—closet-sized rooms, interior walls that streamed water when the roof gutters overflowed, and an attic where pigeons would fly through the holes and get stuck inside.

Even with all the unwelcome surprises, I was happy in that little house. The energy of young love and my newfound joy at being a mother sang happiness and vibrancy into my life. Joel had just been delivered by an Austrian midwife in the hospital down the cobbled street on a cold, windy November night, and Sarah toddled around telling everyone who would listen that "Dod had diven us a baby boy— dust like Desus was when He came to Mary on Christmas!" Having heard the story of Jesus' birth in the dark of our chapel one evening, she was sure that Joel was our own Jesus, and she would look out the window each evening watching for the angels to appear to sing him a song.

On Christmas Eve, we thought our little home had never looked more beautiful. Light from the crimson candles shimmered each time someone rang our bell. Our tiny antique dining table was laden with winter delicacies: red apples, golden pears, and large polished hazelnuts. All our guests would crowd around that table, content to share in the friendly companionship of such a festive evening.

Our motley but happy company included a young Austrian woman whose spouse had just abandoned her for another man; a youthful Taiwanese secretary working for the United Nations; a refugee who had escaped his Middle Eastern country by crossing over the border at night, chased by secret police; and a young missionary from England, lonely on his very first Christmas away from his family. Sarah sat chattering in my lap and talking about the angels. Our live-in friend helped me serve our "shepherds' meal"—potato soup, freshly baked homemade bread, a variety of cheeses, and an assortment of nuts and fruits—and we all sang "Silent Night" as a prayer because it was the only carol everyone knew.

Hearts were opened by the beauty of the meal, and as we all delighted in our feast, we spoke of the shepherds who had received the Good News of Jesus on that first Christmas so long ago. My heart was warmed by the sight of friends from such different cultures sharing our table; I cherished the love that whispered Christ's reality through the moments of the evening.

Our guests spoke four different languages. Multiple denominational persuasions were represented as well: Roman Catholic, *Evangelisch* (Lutheran Reformed), Baptist, and Anglican. Our final guest, an agnostic, listened and looked on with curiosity and an open heart. I remember thinking that this was what heaven would be like—all unified, all tied together by the sharing of friendship and a common love. Here we all celebrated Jesus' first coming, worshiping together from our own traditions but grateful for the Divine Love that had kissed our evening with His presence.

This is the power of the feast. It is no accident that when time is fulfilled, the culmination of the renewing of all things will be a great wedding feast, with Christ as the honored Host. Even in the deepest of winters—physical or spiritual—the embers of faith that burn in our hearts can start a fire of joy if that faith is shared in an intentional celebration together.

As humans we are created in the image of God, whose very nature is relationship and mutual celebration. Each member of the Trinity glories in and celebrates the next; in this reality our model for community is profoundly striking. As we glory in one another and celebrate life—feasting together, sharing songs and stories, encouraging and supporting one another—we are mirroring the very real example of the Father, the Son, and the Holy Spirit.

Let that understanding send you forth in mission to seek out friendship, celebrate well, and feast with passion. May the light of Christ pierce through the darkness of your life, and may your home be filled with the joy of celebration every month of the year.

If you are lonely or struggling, start small. Prepare some food, put on a pot of coffee or tea, invite someone in, and see if that simple act catalyzes renewal in your life. Revel in the other person's life and celebrate him or her. God delights in our presence, and He delights when we enjoy one another's company. Joy is one of the central aspects of the gospel, and for good reason. No matter our circumstances or struggles, God has spoken the light of life into the universe in the person of Christ, and in His work through Christians like us, the world is being made new, one person at a time.

At Home in the Word

1. *"The Word became flesh, and dwelt among us, and we saw His glory, glory as of the only begotten from the Father, full of grace and truth" (John 1:14).*

   a. The term for God taking tangible human form—the Word becoming flesh—is *Incarnation*. Why do you think that God becoming human is such a big deal? What does this reality say to you personally?

   b. This chapter suggests that relationship is part of God's very being—Father, Son, and Holy Spirit interacting and celebrating together. What does this tell us about the importance of our own relationships, of sharing life and celebrating together? Write down at least one idea for celebrating this month with family, friends, and perhaps someone in need of a little community.

2. *"The people who walk in darkness will see a great light; those who live in a dark land, the light will shine on them" (Isaiah 9:2).*

   a. No matter the darkness encroaching upon our lives, God's light is stronger and will always overcome the darkness. Think of a time of darkness in your life, a time when you were living in a "dark land" and desperately in need of warmth and light. How did you find hope during that time?

   b. Write down one or two or three tangible ways you and your family could incarnate God's light for someone who is stuck in some form of darkness—financial trouble, loneliness, confusion. Do you think it's possible to incarnate light to someone else when you yourself are caught up in darkness? Why or why not?

3. *"A child will be born to us, a son will be given to us; and the government will rest on His shoulders; and His name will be called Wonderful Counselor, Mighty God, Eternal Father, Prince of Peace" (Isaiah 9:6).*

   a. Names are very important in Scripture. Christ is given many names, including several in this verse. What "names" do you tend to apply to yourself mentally, and how do you tend to label your family members? Do you see yourself and others as "Beloved of God" or "God's Workmanship"—or are you living under old, tired names of condemnation and guilt? Write down some names for yourself and those you love that reflect who you really are in Christ and God's true attitude toward you. Share them with your family and repeat them often as reminders of your heritage.

b. Jesus is called the Prince of Peace. What are some tangible ways you can incarnate His peace in your home and with your family? Write down three possible ways to cut down on squabbling and conflict.

4. *"O taste and see that the LORD is good; how blessed is the man who takes refuge in Him!" (Psalm 34:8).*

a. God blessed humanity with the ability to use all our senses—to hear, touch, smell, taste, and see—to draw closer to Him. What are some ways that engaging your senses can help you take refuge in God? (Think of taking a walk in the sunshine, drinking a fragrant cup of tea, reading a meaningful book.) List a few specific ideas that help you taste and see that God is good.

b. Meals are such an important part of celebration, especially during the holiday seasons. What can you do to make mealtimes more appealing to the senses? List some specific strategies. (*The Lifegiving Home* is full of ideas.)

Bringing It Home

WHAT IS YOUR BIGGEST CHALLENGE FOR DECEMBER?

Christmas inevitably means many more people in the house, and that in turn means much more cleaning, more cooking, and more conversing to do. Though it keeps me on my toes, I always remind myself what a delightful challenge it is in the end, as the blessing of being surrounded by all my children and friends far outweighs the extra work.

What do you struggle with in December? What are you doing (or could you do) to overcome that struggle?

_____

_____

_____

_____

_____

December Anniversaries, Birthdays, and Holidays

Christmas is more than just a day for our family. It is an entire season—or actually two seasons, because we observe both the quieter Advent season and the entire twelve days of the Christmas season, which begins on Christmas Day.

We start the season off with an Advent wreath, lighting candles each week to represent different ways in which we anticipate Christ's coming. A Clarkson Christmas open house, held at some point in December, is one of our most anticipated events of the year, and we do it in style, inviting friends from near and far. Our Christmas Eve still features the same shepherds' meal we enjoyed so long ago in Vienna—simple dishes enjoyed by candlelight and accompanied by a reading of the shepherds' story in the Gospel of Luke. On Christmas Day we share a grand breakfast together at the Broadmoor, a hundred-year-old five-star hotel down the road from us, before going home to unwrap presents and begin dinner. And even then it's not over, because the celebrations continue through New Year's Day and on until Epiphany on January 6. It's a busy time but a joyful one, and none of us would miss a minute of it.

List your own family events for December:

_____

_____

_____

_____

_____

To Read or Watch in December

Picture Books: The Christmas season has inspired a surprising number of wonderful Christmas books. One of our favorites, Lori Walburg's *The Legend of the Candy Cane* (1997), is a faith-filled account of the spiritual symbolism of the seasonal treat. *The Christmas Miracle of Jonathan Toomey* (1995), by Susan Wojciechowski, is another touching story with beautiful artwork by P. J. Lynch. For a longer list, see *The Lifegiving Home* or our family resource guide at www.lifegivinghome.com.

Literature and Nonfiction: A must-read for the advent season is Charles Dickens's *A Christmas Carol* (1843), a classic work of Victorian England sure to inspire life and light for the season.

Movies and Series: We have so many favorite Christmas movies, but *The Muppet Christmas Carol* (1992) is at the top of our list. This unique version of Dickens's classic story, told as only the Muppets can, is infused with a surprising amount of heart. Our other go-to seasonal films are *Miracle on 34th Street* (we actually prefer the more recent 1994 version) and *The Bishop's Wife* (1947).

Consider which of these or other books, television series, or films you could enjoy with your family in December.

People Priorities for December

December is a month filled with opportunities to host beloved guests. A mother-daughter tea, a dessert potluck with friends ending with a carol sing, and a multifamily progressive dinner are some of the ways our family celebrates people in December. I especially enjoy seeing one of my oldest friends, Gwen, who worked with me behind the Iron Curtain in Poland with Campus Crusade for Christ (now Cru).

She always visits our family in the weeks before Christmas Day. I relish spending time with her, enjoying her friendship and camaraderie and hearing all about her life.

What people do you plan to prioritize in December?
With whom do you most want to share the wonder of the season?

_____

_____

_____

_____

_____

An Invitation to Create a History of Goodness in Your Home

Writing these two books about home—*The Lifegiving Home* and *The Lifegiving Home Experience*—has stretched my own heart and mind to realize more clearly than ever before how important the building of home is, not only to our own emotional and spiritual health but also to the current generation of children and adults. When we have a place to rest our heads each night with the expectation of love and acceptance, good food, encouragement, and the safety to be ourselves, then we have the foundations of goodness from which to live all of life.

Years ago I read these words somewhere: "The way the home goes will determine the way culture is shaped: in faith, morals, spiritual strength, and foundations for life." Home matters, in other words, and not just to the ones who live there. The reach of a lifegiving home is much, much wider than its walls. It literally can change the world.

Shaping such a home and building such a legacy of love and faith requires someone to take responsibility for doing just that. If you are reading this book, that person is probably you. It is my hope and prayer that it will validate the hard but important work that you are doing; suggest some fun and meaningful ways to shape your family's life together; and—most important—inspire you to come up with your own traditions, disciplines, and memories. The legacy of a lifegiving home is yours to create for those you love. I pray that God blesses you and your precious ones inside your walls with His favor. May you rely on His love, His goodness, and His strength to face each day with faith.

Notes and Ideas

_____

_____

_____

_____

_____

_____

_____

_____

About the Authors

Sally Clarkson is the beloved author of multiple books, including *Own Your Life* and *Desperate* (with Sarah Mae). As a mother of four, she has inspired thousands of mothers through Whole Heart Ministries (www.wholeheart.org), which she founded with her husband, Clay, in 1998. Since then, she has advocated relentlessly for the power of motherhood and the influence of home through her Mom Heart conferences (www.momheart.com), speaking to audiences on several continents. Sally encourages many through her blogs and websites—www.sallyclarkson.com and www.lifegivinghome.com (the companion site to this book)—as well as through her e-books and live webinars.

From the soaring, cinematic sounds of his film music to his melodic, pensive piano works, **Joel Clarkson** is an award-winning composer who is known for the vibrant colors of sound he paints with his music. Joel's composition is often focused on film scores, and he has provided original music for numerous feature and short films in addition to orchestrating and conducting for many different genres and settings. He has also received high praise as a concert composer and orchestrator, and his creative contributions to concert music have been heard around the world to great acclaim.

Joel has provided his expertise in many other artistic environments, including the audiobook world, where he has delighted listeners near and far as an engaging voice artist, and also in nonfiction publishing, where he has collaborated as a creative contributor and editor for numerous books. Joel was born in Vienna, Austria, and received his undergraduate degree from the Berklee College of Music, summa cum laude. He currently finds his home in the shadow of the beautiful Rocky Mountains in Monument, Colorado. For more information, please visit www.joelclarkson.com.